Contents

The Key begins on page 97 of the With Key edition.

Acknowledgements

The author and publishers are grateful to the following for permission to reproduce extracts and adaptations of copyright material:

The BBC for the extract from 'Stressed out in Sweden' by Rosie Goldsmith (page 28).

Far & Near Travel Magazine (www.far-and-near.com) for the adapted extract from 'Historic Antigua' by A.K. Lee (page 44).

Lorraine Gregoire for the adapted version of *The Big Blue Shirt* (page 80).

The Guardian for the extract from 'By gum, here's something for the memory to start chewing on', © Helen Carter (page 24), and for 'The future is purple', © The Guardian 2002 (page 72).

The Institute for Social Inventions for the extract from the www.internet-free-day.org home page (page 8).

OK PetGazette for the extract from 'The shepherd's dog' by Hugh Jones, © Ashworth Publishing LLC 2000–01 (pages 56–7).

Time Warner Books UK for the extract from *Weird Weather* by Paul Simons (pages 60–61).

Weekend Magazine for 'A short history of frozen food' by Julian Champkin (page 33).

Every effort has been made to trace and contact the copyright holders of material used in this book. The publishers apologise for any inadvertent errors or omissions, which they will be pleased to rectify at the earliest opportunity.

Illustrations by: Josephine Blake (pages 80, 81, 82), Martyn Ford (pages 8, 48) and David Woodroffe (pages 34, 35, 60, 69)

Photographs by permission of: imagestate.com (pages 16, 32, 44), Marinepics Limited (page 40) and popperfoto.com (pages 56, 68)

Cover design by Vasso Varvaki

DEVELOPING INTERMEDIATE VOCABULARY

SIMON HAINES

GEORGIAN PRESS

Georgian Press (Jersey) Limited
Pirouet House
Union Street
St Helier
Jersey JE4 8ZQ
Channel Islands

© Simon Haines 2003

First published by Georgian Press (Jersey) Limited 2003

ISBN 1-873630-36-0 (without key)
ISBN 1-873630-37-9 (with key)

Produced by AMR Limited

Printed in Egypt by International Printing House

Introduction

The purpose of *Developing Intermediate Vocabulary* is to enable intermediate-level students to discover, learn and practise words and phrases in authentic contexts. Learners using the book will develop an awareness of a wide range of vocabulary, including collocation, word-building, topic vocabulary, and related words.

The book is suitable for use in the classroom or for homework. The With Key edition is essential if the book is to be used for self-study.

How the book is organised

There are 20 four-page topic-based units, followed by five Review units. The topic-based units are not grouped or sequenced in any particular way, so they may be studied in any order. If the book is being used in conjunction with a general English coursebook, it might be possible for teachers to choose units to complement coursebook topics.

Review units
Each Review unit recycles and consolidates some of the most useful words and phrases from the group of four units it relates to.

Collocation lists
On pages 93 and 94 there are lists of collocations, which are cross-referenced to the main units.

Index
Pages 95 and 96 contain a detailed Index of exercises dealing with particular vocabulary items and topics.

Key
The With Key edition contains answers to all the exercises.

How each unit is organised

Each unit is based on a text of 250–350 words in length from an authentic source. Texts are of different types, including magazine articles, newspaper stories, emails and short stories. A small number of the texts are written in American English. Units follow this basic pattern:

Introduction
This introduces key vocabulary from the text which follows. Students match selected words and phrases with their meanings, checking in a dictionary any they do not already know.

Reading
Students read the text and fill the gaps with correct words and phrases from the Introduction. In some units a short comprehension exercise follows this gap-filling task.

Following the reading are a variety of exercise types, all based on vocabulary occurring in the text. In addition there are **Extension** exercises which further develop other related vocabulary. The final exercise in each unit is either a **Practice** or a **Puzzle**. Both these recycle words and phrases from the unit.

The following are exercise types which occur frequently throughout the book.

Related words
A table, usually with the headings *noun, verb, adjective* and *adverb*, contains a number of words from the reading text. Students complete the remaining gaps in the table with related words. See Exercise C on page 9 for an example.

Collocation

The purpose of the numerous collocation exercises is to draw students' attention to pairs of words which are commonly used together. These are of various types:

* Verb + noun   *to lose your temper*
* Adjective + noun   *an expensive mistake*
* Verb + adverb   *to sleep lightly*

Students match appropriate pairs of words, then use the collocations they have formed to complete gapped sentences.

Topic vocabulary

Some students find it helpful to learn words in thematic groups. So, if a reading text contains a number of words or phrases related to a particular subject, one of the exercises may focus on this thematic vocabulary. For example, Unit 10, *A journey to remember*, groups travel nouns together.

Phrasal verbs

A number of units include phrasal verb exercises. These generally focus on one particular verb, for example, *carry, set* or *turn*.

Idioms

The idiom exercises are of different types. They may focus on particular words used idiomatically, e.g. **cut** *someone dead*, **cut** *corners*. They may deal with word types such as adjectives, e.g. **thick***-skinned,* *out of* **thin** *air.* Or the focus may be thematic, as in the exercise on animal idioms: *an early* **bird***, a dark* **horse***,* etc.

Word building

The word-building exercises draw attention to particular features of words. For example:

* Prefixes and suffixes (e.g. **re***wind,* **low***-fat, duty-***free**)
* Noun endings, as in words for jobs (e.g. act**or**, econom**ist** , music**ian**)
* Adjective endings (e.g. bor**ed** / bor**ing**)
* Verbs ending in -en (e.g. sharp**en**, wid**en)**
* Adjectives starting with a- (e.g. **a***wake,* **a***sleep*)

Other vocabulary exercises

There are various other exercises which occur occasionally, including:

* British and American English (e.g. *rubbish / trash*)
* Confusing words (e.g. *house / home*)
* Formal and informal words (e.g. *injured / hurt*)
* Compound nouns (e.g. *street corner*)
* Compound adjectives (e.g. *long-legged*)
* Homophones (e.g. *our / hour*)

These, and many other exercises which focus on vocabulary items specific to particular units, are listed in the Index on pages 95–6.

Extension exercises

These develop an aspect of vocabulary which has featured in a previous exercise. For example, in the verb-noun collocation exercise on page 10, students learn that the verb *lose* is used with the following nouns and phrases:
a chance / contact with someone / an election / interest in something / your job / sight of / your temper / your way.

Extension 2, which follows, focuses on three verbs which are used as the opposites of *lose:*
find / keep / win.

Notes to teachers

If you are using this book in class with your students, remember that units can be done in any order, as texts and exercises are not graded in any way. Choose texts or topics that you think your students will find interesting or useful.

Each unit ends with a final practice exercise, in the form of a short gapped text or puzzle, which recycles vocabulary from the unit. These would make ideal homework exercises. The Review units could be set as occasional tests.

Although the exercises are designed to be done by students working individually, you could ask students to work in pairs on certain exercises. Section A, Introduction, would be suitable for this, as students are encountering a new topic and a new text for the first time. One way of approaching pairwork is to get students to work individually in the first instance, and then to compare their answers with a partner, before a final check in the Key or with the teacher.

Notes to students working alone

The units in this book can be used in any order. Choose texts or topics that you think you will find interesting and useful.

You probably already have your own favourite way of recording and learning vocabulary, but if you don't, here are a number of ways you could try:

- Divide a notebook into several sections. For example, you could use the headings

  TOPICS   VERB + NOUN COLLOCATIONS   WORD-BUILDING   PHRASAL VERBS

  Each time you come across words you want to learn, list them in the appropriate section of your notebook. Try to learn ten new words or combinations of words each day.

- Design a 'spidergram' to include a set of words you would like to remember. These work particularly well for groups of words related by topic. Example:

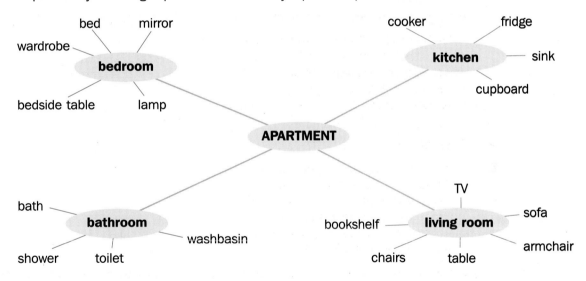

- Write sentences incorporating the words or phrases you want to remember, then make a tape recording of these sentences. Listen to the tape from time to time and repeat the sentences until you feel you know them. (This method works best if you write your own sentences, but if you are short of time use the sentences from the book.)

- From each unit, choose 10 words or phrases you think you will find useful. Write them down and stick them somewhere you will see them every day, for example on a noticeboard at home, on the fridge, or even on a mirror you look in regularly. Every time you see them, say them aloud and check you know the meanings. Think of different situations in which you could use them.

And finally ...
The main purpose of this book is to help you develop your vocabulary. We hope you will find the texts and the exercises interesting and useful. Try to use words and phrases you have learned from the book as often as possible – in fact whenever you are speaking or writing English. Remember, it is only by using new words and phrases that you will really learn them.

A day without the Internet

A Introduction

1 These words and phrases are from the article below. Try to match them with their meanings.

a	*big business*	1	something that happens
b	*controversial*	2	unhealthy, low quality, bad for you
c	*event*	3	a person who studies something to discover new information
d	*isolate*	4	a device for controlling a computer
e	*junk (food)*	5	not actively
f	*mouse*	6	causing disagreement and discussion
g	*passively*	7	not real, only on a computer or the Internet
h	*researcher*	8	dangerous
i	*risky*	9	powerful companies and financial organisations
j	*virtual*	10	to keep separate from things or people

2 Check in a dictionary the meaning of any of these words you do not understand.

B Reading

Read the article and fill each gap with a word or phrase from **A1**.

Put down your mouse

An Internet organisation is trying to persuade people to take part in *International Internet-Free Day*, which would be held every year on the last weekend in January. The idea is that people will leave the **(a)** _____ world and go out into the real world. One supporter of the idea said, 'The Internet can be like addictive **(b)** _____: food you can never get enough of but which you don't really want.'

A spokesman for the Internet-Free Day team explained, 'The Internet **(c)** _____s people socially and damages their eyesight. That is what **(d)** _____ has done with it. It was never meant to be like this. The Internet began as a quick and simple way for **(e)** _____s to communicate and exchange information.'

'But it's so easy to get addicted to a half-life in a virtual world, and to lose touch with your family, friends and neighbours. Human beings need contact with the real world. Email and the Internet are just not enough.'

So, put down your **(f)** _____ and turn off your computer. The real world is open all day every day and welcomes visitors. It offers you the chance to feel human again. An Internet-free day will give you back your real life.

Imagine your perfect day, suggest the idea to some friends and find an exciting **(g)** _____ to take part in. Then go out into the world outside your window, and make your perfect day a reality!

Here are some ideas:

- Organise a *Dice Day*. Write down half a dozen unusual things your group could do on the day, number these things from 1 to 6, then throw a dice. You have to agree to do whichever activity the dice chooses.

- Or choose a less **(h)** _____ activity: go for a country walk, visit an art gallery or museum, have a discussion about a(n) **(i)** _____ subject. Anything as long as it involves more than just **(j)** _____ consuming, watching or listening.

C Related words

1 Fill the gaps in this chart with words related to the words given. Sometimes there are two words in one group. (X = no useful word at this level.)

Noun	Verb	Adjective	Adverb
a _____	X	real	_____
b _____ _____ *	X	addictive	X
c _____	damage	_____	X
d _____	communicate	_____	_____
e contact	_____	X	X
f _____ visitor*	_____	X	X
g _____	_____	perfect	_____
h _____	_____	exciting _____	X
i _____	_____	risky	_____

These words refer to people.

2 Fill the gaps in these sentences with words you have added to the chart.
   a A telly _____ is someone who can't stop watching television.
   b If you drink and drive, there's a _____ that you will lose your driving licence.
   c Next time you're on a _____ to London, you must come and see us again.
   d I know I'm not very _____ this evening, but I've had a hard day and I don't feel like talking.
   e When I fell over I hurt my leg, but I don't think I've done any serious _____.
   f If I were you I'd _____ the police and report the accident straightaway.
   g She's really _____ about starting her new job. She's been looking forward to it for weeks.

D The suffix *-free*

An *Internet-free day* is a day without the Internet. Match these adjectives with the suffix *-free* with nouns they could describe.

alcohol-free   duty-free   fat-free   lead-free   rent-free   trouble-free

accommodation / cigarettes / drink / goods / holiday / journey / lager / paint / petrol / wine / yoghurt

EXTENSION 1

1 Addictions

An alcoholic is someone who is addicted to alcohol. What are these people addicted to?
a chocoholic   a shopaholic   a workaholic

2 *Go for*

The article suggests that people *go for a walk*. Which of these can we *go for*?

> *a bicycle ride / a drink / a drive / a football match / a picnic / a run /*
> *a shop / a swim*

E Verb-noun collocations

1 The verbs below are from the article. Which nouns or phrases in the box can follow them? Make four lists. (Some nouns or phrases can follow more than one verb.)

exchange   hold   lose   offer

> *advice / contact with someone / a conversation / someone a drink / an election /*
> *an explanation / glances / greetings / ideas / information / interest in / your job /*
> *someone a lift / a meeting / an opinion / phone numbers / sight of / your temper /*
> *your way*

2 Find the best endings for these sentence beginnings, and fill each gap with the correct form of one of the verbs from above.

Beginnings	Endings
a I've been out of work for over a year, then last week the phone rang and ...	1 there's no need to _____ your temper.
b We had to postpone the meeting because so many people were ill, so ...	2 we must _____ addresses and phone numbers.
c I wasn't trying to annoy you –	3 I _____ my way.
d Sorry I'm late. I don't know the town very well and ...	4 someone _____ me a job.
e Can I _____ you a drink?	5 He never _____ an opinion.
f Let's keep in touch. Before you go, ...	6 Who do you think will win?
g They are _____ the election soon.	7 We've got beer, wine or orange juice.
h It's difficult to know what he thinks.	8 we're _____ it next week instead.

EXTENSION 2

1 Opposites of *lose*

What are the opposites of the *lose* collocations from E1? Make expressions with these verbs.

find   keep   win

a _____ your temper   d _____ in contact with

b _____ your way   e _____ an election

c _____ your job

2 Collocations with *change*

Answer the questions with words or phrases from the box.

> *channels / your clothes / currency / jobs / your mind / the subject / trains*

a What do you sometimes have to change when you travel by rail?
b What could you change if you were too warm or too cold?
c What do you sometimes need to change when you go from one country to another – so that you can buy things?
d What do you change when you alter your opinion?
e What do you change when you want to talk about something different?
f What do you change when you're fed up with the work you are doing?
g What do you change when you want to watch a different TV programme?

F Phrasal verbs with *turn*

The article tells you to **turn off** your computer.

1 Match these *turn* verbs with one or more of meanings a–g.

turn down   turn off   turn on   turn up

a arrive at a place or event
b increase sound or heat from something like a radio or a cooker
c leave one road to go along another
d move a switch so that something starts working
e move a switch so that something stops working
f reduce sound or heat from something like a radio or a cooker
g refuse an offer or the person who makes it

2 Complete each sentence with the correct form of a *turn* verb from **F1**.

a I can't work because the TV's too loud. Please _____ it _____ .
b Go along the motorway for about 10 kilometres and then _____ _____ when you see signs for London.
c It was a great game, but unfortunately only a few people _____ _____ .
d I'm really cold. Can you _____ the heating _____ , please?
e He applied for a job as a policeman, but they _____ him _____ .

G Practice

Read this letter from someone reacting to the idea of an Internet-free day. Fill the gaps with words and phrases from sections **A–F** above.

> I think the idea of an Internet-free day is really brilliant. Lots of my friends – myself included – are completely **(a)** _____ to their computers and spend hours and hours every day in their own **(b)** _____ world. Another friend just can't stop working – he admits himself that he's a **(c)** _____ . So I am definitely going to **(d)** _____ my mouse, **(e)** _____ my computer and **(f)** _____ my friends to persuade them to get involved in an **(g)** _____ or activity where we can actually do something **(h)** _____ for a change. We're thinking about **(i)** _____ a bike ride or perhaps helping to tidy up the local park. I'm not very brave, so I don't want to do anything too **(j)** _____ .

2 The future of music

A Introduction

1 These words are from the article below. Try to match them with their meanings.

a	*accessible*	1	involving large numbers of people / the majority
b	*consumer*	2	able to change easily
c	*download*	3	the amount something is worth
d	*duplicate*	4	melodies
e	*flexible*	5	to choose
f	*luxury*	6	a person who buys and uses products
g	*mass*	7	to copy from the Internet to a computer
h	*select*	8	easy to get
i	*tunes*	9	great comfort or wealth
j	*value*	10	to copy, to reproduce

2 Check in a dictionary the meaning of any of these words you do not understand.

B Reading

1 Read the article and fill each gap with the correct form of a word from **A1**.

Digital and free

The fact that technology is changing music is nothing new. The arrival of the phonograph in the late 19th century made it possible to **(a)** _____ performances, with the result that there is no music made today that has not been shaped by the fact of recording.

As recording technology spread throughout the world, it had some surprising effects. Folk **(b)** _____, for example, which had always been **(c)** _____, changing with each performance, were transformed by recording into fixed songs that could be exactly repeated.

Consumerism grew in the last century as technology improved. What **(d)** _____ consumed – whether books, CDs or videos – were exact copies. The ability to make huge quantities of copies was the key ingredient of **(e)** _____ culture.

The massive upset that music is now experiencing is the change from analogue copies to digital copies. The analogue copies of the industrial age were perfect and cheap. The information age is driven by digital copies, which are perfect and **free.**

Of course, it's not just music that is being copied for free: it is text, pictures, movies, entire websites. But the moment something becomes free, its **(f)** _____ changes. When electric lighting was new and expensive, the poor burned candles. When electricity became easily **(g)** _____ and cheap, candles at dinner became a sign of **(h)** _____. Now, the only truly valuable things are those which cannot be copied.

What kinds of things can't be copied? A friend may pass on a recording by your favourite group, but if you pay, the group will e-mail it to you seconds after the performance. Similarly, you may **(i)** _____ the music of a rock band from the Internet, but the only way to get the full details of each track is to contact the band and pay.

Free music brings other problems. No matter what your tastes, there are not enough hours in a lifetime to listen to more than a tiny fraction of the music which is recorded each year. So people will pay to have someone **(j)** _____, edit and present the music to them in an easy and fun manner. Music will continue to be sold, because it will be easier to buy music you really like than to find it for free.

2 Read the article again and decide if these statements are true (T) false (F).

    a The phonograph was invented during the last century.   **T / F**

    b Recording technology helped folk music to become more flexible.   **T / F**

    c Analogue copies were cheaper than digital copies.   **T / F**

    d Things that can be copied are worth less than things that cannot be copied.   **T / F**

    e The writer predicts that in the future nobody will pay for music.   **T / F**

C Related words

1 Fill the gaps in this chart with words related to words given. Sometimes there are two words in one group. (X = no useful word at this level.)

Noun	Verb	Adjective
a _____	_____	accessible

b electricity
    _____ *
	X	electrical
		    _____

c _____	_____	industrial _____ (country)
d luxury	X	_____
e performance _____ *	_____	X
f _____	repeat	_____
g _____	select	_____
h technology _____ *	X	_____
i _____	transform	X
j value	_____	valuable

These words refer to people.

2 Fill the gaps in these sentences with the correct form of words you have added to the chart.

    a The car _____ used to employ millions of workers. Now a lot of the work is done by robots.

    b Have you ever _____ in front of a live audience?

    c My best friend's family is very wealthy – they live in a really _____ house.

    d In the twentieth century steam trains were replaced by _____ trains.

    e If you want a new car, look in the local paper – there is a huge _____ to choose from.

    f This job is terribly _____. I have to do the same thing hundreds of times a day.

EXTENSION: Adjective pairs

Look at these pairs of adjectives and their meanings, then choose the correct word in sentences **a–f**.

Adjective	Meaning	Example
economic	relating to business or industry	economic theories
economical	cheap, not expensive to run	an economical heating system
electric	using electricity	an electric cooker
electrical	concerned with electricity	an electrical engineer
historic	important, significant	a historic speech
historical	happening in the past	a historical event

a This is a very *economic / economical* car. It does 20 kilometres to the litre.
b Tomorrow's meeting between the two leaders will be a *historic / historical* occasion.
c In the future, *electric / electrical* cars will be more common.
d The government is bringing in a new *economic / economical* policy.
e My brother is the manager of an *electric / electrical* store.
f I've just read a fantastic *historic / historical* novel. It's set during the French Revolution.

D Adjective-noun collocations

1 Which nouns in the box can follow these adjectives from the article? Make four lists.

cheap   expensive   free   valuable

*experience / fares / gift / holiday / imitation / information /
mistake / newspaper / seat / ticket*

2 Complete these sentences using adjective-noun collocations from **D1**.

a When you order your first three books from the club, we will send you a(n) _____ _____ worth at least £10.
b That's not a real diamond ring. It's just a(n) _____ _____.
c Some companies are prepared to pay a lot of money for _____ _____ about their competitors.
d Buying that second-hand car was a(n) _____ _____. It's broken down three times already.
e Most _____ _____s are full of advertisements and contain hardly any news.
f For many people, going to university is a very _____ _____'. They learn a lot about the world and themselves.
g During its Shakespeare season, the theatre is offering _____ _____ to students.
h For their honeymoon they went on a really _____ _____ to the Seychelles.

E Music words

1 The words in the box are all related to music and recording. Group them under the four headings which follow. One example of each is given.

*band / cassette / CD / composer / group / folk / instrument / jazz / mini-disc / opera /
orchestra / performance / pop / rhythm / rock / singer / song / studio / track / tune*

Kinds of music	People	Words connected with recording	Other words
folk	*group*	*CD*	*instrument*

2 Check in a dictionary the meaning of any of these words you do not understand.

3 Add any more words you know to the lists.

F Word groups

Here are some groups of words. In each group, one word is a general word and the others are examples of this general word.
Example:

> *gold / metal / silver / steel*
>
> **Metal** is the general word; *gold*, *silver* and *steel* are different kinds of metal.

Which are the general words in these groups?

a *electricity / energy / gas / nuclear power / solar power*
b *cinema / entertainment / theatre / television*
c *breakfast / dinner / lunch / meal / supper*
d *century / month / time / week / year*
e *cassette / CD / DVD / mini-disc / recording*

G Puzzle

Find the following words in this puzzle. They can be horizontal, vertical or diagonal.

a Two 'price' adjectives with opposite meanings
b Someone who buys things
c Another word for *choose*
d Traditional musicians make this kind of music.
e Able to change easily
f Two modern jobs
g A melody
h An adjective related to *economy*
i The noun related to *repeat*
j The adjective related to *luxury*
k A late meal
l A recording of film or television

E	L	U	N	C	T	U	N	E	P	I	T
R	X	F	L	E	X	I	B	L	E	L	E
E	C	P	R	O	D	F	V	S	C	U	C
C	H	H	E	N	E	O	A	E	O	X	H
O	A	S	E	N	N	L	L	L	N	U	N
N	C	R	U	A	S	K	U	E	S	R	O
O	C	H	I	P	P	I	M	C	U	I	L
M	E	A	S	I	P	V	V	T	M	O	O
I	S	T	I	L	T	E	I	E	E	U	G
C	T	V	I	D	E	O	R	N	R	S	I
P	R	E	P	E	T	I	T	I	O	N	S
E	L	E	C	T	R	I	C	I	A	N	T

3 Mobile phones

A Introduction

1 a Which of these does not have a *screen*?

    A a television   **B** a watch   **C** a cinema   **D** a mobile phone

  b Which of these does not have *keys*?

    A a video recorder   **B** a piano   **C** a computer   **D** a mobile phone

2 Complete sentences **a–j** with words from the box. You may have to change the words slightly. (Use your dictionary to check the meanings of any words you are not sure of.)

> character / communicate / company / compose / emergency / peaktime /
> pre-paid / ring / text

a _____ calls are the most expensive because that's the most popular time for people to use their phones.

b When mobile phones were first introduced, many people only used them in _____ .

c For many young people, mobile phones are the most popular way of _____ with friends.

d It can be embarrassing if your phone _____ when you are in a public place.

e If you are musical, you can _____ your own ring tones.

f The name for a written phone message is a _____ message.

g I couldn't understand the notice because it was written in Chinese _____ .

h Vodaphone and Orange are two well-known mobile phone _____ .

i _____ calls are those you pay for before you make them.

B Reading

Read the article and fill each gap with the correct form of a word from **A1** or **A2**.

Look who's talking

When parents buy their children a mobile phone, they probably imagine them on a street corner somewhere, needing to phone home. They intend it for **(a)** _____ and for short, important calls. They do not expect them to send silly messages to their friends in the school classroom. This is **(b)** _____ messaging, or 'texting', which allows kids to **(c)** _____ with each other easily and quickly. According to phone **(d)** _____ , it's a rapidly growing habit.

To a 16-year-old, the attraction of text messaging over old-fashioned phone calls is obvious: it is silent and secret. It is also cheap. Most British under-18s now have mobiles, and many of these phones are on **(e)** _____ packages, which means that parents have some control over how much their children spend. A **(f)** _____ call might cost 30 pence, but for about 10 pence they can type in a message of up to 160 **(g)** _____ and send it anywhere in the country.

15-year-old Sunita goes to a school in London where teachers take away mobiles if they **(h)** _____ during lessons. 'Texting is good fun,' she says. 'Nobody can see which **(i)** _____ you're pressing, so they've no idea what you're writing.'

A survey of 10- to 21-year-olds asked them why they liked text messaging. 'Fun' came at the top of the list; then 'cheap', 'silent, 'private' and 'immediate'.

'Mobile phones are like toys,' says Nigel O'Brien of *Mobile Choice* magazine. 'You can **(j)** _____ your own ring tone, send picture messages, play games on their little **(k)** _____ , or even programme them to ring out your favourite pop song.' And soon, of course, more of us will be using them to take and send instant photos too!

C Verb-noun collocations

1 The verbs below are from the article. Which nouns in the box can follow them? Make four lists. (Some nouns can follow more than one verb.)

play   press   send   spend

> a button / a CD / chess / energy / football / a key / a letter / a message / money / the piano / a present / a signal / a switch / time / a trick on someone

2 Find the best endings for these sentence beginnings, and fill each gap with the correct form of one of the verbs from **C1**.

Beginnings	Endings
a It's really easy to start the computer –	**1** It's someone _____ the violin.
b I can't afford to come out tonight –	**2** I _____ it by airmail.
c What's that dreadful noise?	**3** Why don't you have a break for lunch?
d Let's _____ a trick on your brother.	**4** you just _____ this button.
e They should have got my letter by now –	**5** Yes, but I haven't _____ for months.
f If you want to get rid of what you've written, ...	**6** _____ the delete key.
g Are you still interested in golf?	**7** Good idea! Let's hide his car keys.
h You've _____ all morning writing that report.	**8** I _____ all my money.

EXTENSION 1

You can **kill** time, **save** time, **spend** time or **waste** time. What other nouns can go with these verbs? Tick the spaces in this table.

	time	energy	food	your life	a person	money
kill	✔					
save	✔					
spend	✔					
waste	✔					

D Compound nouns

1 A compound noun is a noun with two or more parts. Here are some examples from the article.

> *mobile phone / street corner / text messaging / school classroom / phone companies / phone calls / under-18s / picture message / pop songs*

How are these compound nouns made? Match each noun in the box with one of these descriptions:

- noun + noun
- noun + noun + noun
- noun + -*ing*
- adjective + noun
- preposition + noun

2 We often use compound nouns instead of longer phrases. For example:

a street corner = the corner of a street
under-18s = people who are under 18 years old

Make compound nouns to use instead of these phrases:

a a conversation on the phone
b people who are over 30 years old
c the tone which a phone makes when it rings
d a phone box in a public place
e a message on a machine which answers the phone

E Related words

1 Fill gaps in this chart with words related to the words given. Sometimes there are two words in one group. (X = no useful word at this level.)

Noun	Verb	Adjective	Adjective with opposite meaning
a _____ _____	X	mobile	_____
b _____	imagine	_____ _____	_____
c _____	intend	_____	_____
d _____	_____	growing	X
e attraction	_____	_____	_____
f _____		silent	X
g _____ _____	X	secret	X
h _____	X	private	X
i _____	X	immediate	X

2 Fill the gaps in these sentences with words you have added to the chart.

    a I'm sorry I offended you. It wasn't _____ .

    b Recently there has been a dramatic _____ in the use of mobile phones.

    c I can't _____ her attention even though I've been calling to her for several minutes.

    d I can't concentrate on reading unless there is complete _____ in the room.

    e When I was a child, I had a(n) _____ friend who lived under my bed. At the time, I really thought he was real.

    f When they become famous, many pop stars and film stars lose their _____ .

EXTENSION 2: Adjectives and their opposites

Here are some pairs of adjectives with opposite meanings. Notice how the second word is different from the first.

mobile / immobile
legal / illegal
responsible / irresponsible
polite / impolite

Now replace the adjectives in these phrases with words which have the opposite meanings.

    a *regular* mealtimes
    b a *patient* teacher
    c *legible* handwriting (*legible* = possible to read)
    d a *mature* teenager (*mature* = grown up)
    e a *relevant* question

F Practice

Read this summary of a report from an anti-smoking organisation. Fill the gaps with words or phrases from sections **A–E** above.

Smoking and mobiles

Doctors think that the recent steady **(a)** _____ in the use of mobile phones among the **(b)** _____ -18s may be one explanation for the dramatic decrease in teenage smoking since 1996. Experts are suggesting that mobile phones may meet some of the same needs as cigarettes for this age group. It's more than just something to do with the hands. Mobiles are cool – they're **(c)** _____ because they are adult. Like cigarettes, they help young people to create a self-image and to feel part of a group. If they see their friends **(d)** _____ with each other, either by **(e)** _____ them or by **(f)** _____ them text **(g)** _____ , they will almost certainly regard mobile phones as essential.

    With pay-as-you-go mobile phones, young people are even **(h)** _____ their money in the same way and at the same places as they would if they were buying cigarettes. Some can't afford to do both, others might get all they want from having a mobile, and for them smoking may become unimportant. For some of today's teenagers, smoking might even seem like 'old technology'.

A Introduction

1 These words and phrases are from the article below. Try to match them with their meanings.

a	*drop*	1	to object to, to complain about
b	*furious*	2	to drive faster than the limit
c	*gesture*	3	to go down, to fall
d	*major*	4	where people live
e	*pack*	5	with nothing to show its identity
f	*protest against*	6	a movement of hands
g	*rage*	7	a group that moves around together
h	*residential*	8	great anger
i	*speed*	9	extremely angry
j	*unmarked*	10	main, important

2 Check in a dictionary the meaning of any of these words you do not understand.

B Reading

1 Read the article from an American newspaper and fill the gaps with the correct form of words from **A1**.

Slow down! This ain't the Mainland!

Bumper stickers in Hawaii say "Slow down! This ain't the Mainland!" But now drivers **(a)** _____ (*3 words*) a programme forcing them to drive more slowly. Recently the state began using digital cameras – operated from **(b)** _____ vans – to catch drivers who **(c)** _____ and run red lights on certain state roads and highways.

The response has been rapid. Several thousand **(d)** _____ drivers have bought illegal covers to hide their license plates. They have written letters to the local papers trying to persuade people not to pay their tickets. Cellphone brigades call morning radio shows to tell them where the vans are, and there are hundreds of reports of drivers making angry **(e)** _____ and even throwing trash at the vans.

One group says the problem is not speeding, but the speed limits. At 55 miles per hour, Hawaii's speed limit is the lowest in the USA. On many **(f)** _____ highways, which often go past schools and **(g)** _____ areas, the limit **(h)** _____ to 45 or 35 m.p.h.

Some officials are even saying that the program may be working too well. "People are now driving too slowly," said a spokeswoman for the City of Honolulu. "They're driving in **(i)** _____ so their plates can't be seen by the cameras. There are people who speed around these packs. And, of course, the vans themselves are being attacked by drivers."

The scheme has caused such **(j)** _____ that some lawmakers are thinking about abandoning it. They say it makes people drive badly.

In one respect, though, the program is a clear success. In its first eight days, it produced nearly 1,300 traffic citations. Normally, there are about 800 citations in an eight-day period.

2 How much do you remember about the article? Answer these questions, then read the article again to check your answers.

    a Where are the digital cameras?
    b Who do the angry motorists telephone to say where the cameras are?
    c What is the speed limit in Hawaii?
    d How do motorists try to avoid the cameras?
    e How many speeding motorists did the cameras catch in the first eight days?

C Strong adjectives

1 The motorists of Hawaii were *furious* about the speed cameras. *Furious* is stronger than *angry*.
Put these sets of adjectives in order, starting with the weakest and ending with the strongest. Use a dictionary to check your ideas.

    a *angry / furious / irritated*
    b *cold / cool / freezing*
    c *good / excellent / satisfactory*
    d *exhausted / sleepy / tired*
    e *amazing / surprising / unexpected*

2 Now complete these sentences with one of the 'strongest' adjectives from **C1**.

    a I've been working since 6 o'clock this morning. I'm completely _____!
    b The heating broke down last night. I woke up absolutely _____!
    c The firework display was totally _____. I've never seen anything like it.
    d It was the fourth time that week that the train had been late. The passengers were absolutely _____!
    e He got 98% for his assignment. His work was simply _____!

EXTENSION 1: Related words

What are the nouns related to these adjectives from **C1**?

a *amazing*	_____		**e** *good*	_____
b *cool*	_____		**f** *irritated*	_____
c *excellent*	_____		**g** *satisfactory*	_____
d *furious*	_____		**h** *surprising*	_____

D American English

1 The article you have just read is from the *New York Times* and is written in American English. Match these words from the article with their British English equivalents.

    a *cellphone*   **1** number plate
    b *citation*   **2** rubbish
    c *highway*   **3** summons (an order to appear in a law court)
    d *license plate*   **4** to cross, to drive through
    e *run (red lights)*   **5** mobile
    f *trash*   **6** main road

2 There are some spelling differences between British and American English. For example, *program* in American English is spelt *programme* in British English. Can you fill the gaps in this chart with the missing words?

American	British
a program	programme
b center	_____
c _____	humour
d license (*noun*)	_____
e _____	catalogue
f traveled	_____

E Verb-noun collocations: *Make* and *do*

1 Some of the drivers in Hawaii *make angry gestures* at the unmarked vans. Which words and phrases in the box follow *make* and which follow *do*? Write two lists of ten words and phrases in your exercise book.

> your best / business with someone / the cooking / a crossword / damage / a decision / an effort / exercises / housework / a job / a mistake / a noise / someone an offer / a painting / a phone call / progress / room for something / the shopping / a suggestion / trouble

make	do

2 Now complete these conversations using expressions with *make* or *do* from **E1**.

a We've run out of food. Shall I go to the supermarket and _____?

b I'm sorry, it's all my fault. I _____ a terrible _____.

c If you want to pass your exams, you'll have to _____ a much bigger _____.

d Last night's storm _____ a lot of _____ to our roof. It'll need replacing.

e You'll have to move the piano if you want to _____ the new TV.

f Can I _____? Why don't you learn to drive? You'd have an easier life.

g The people next door _____ so much _____ last night that I couldn't get to sleep.

EXTENSION 2: Meanings of *make* and *do*

The verbs *make* and *do* have many meanings. What do they mean in sentences a–f? Choose synonyms from the box.

> come to / cut or style / earn / equal / spend / travel at

a My brother *makes* about £1000 a week.

b The driver admitted to the police that he had been *doing* over 200 kilometres an hour.

c He *did* five years in prison for burglary.

d Fifty-three and forty-seven *makes* exactly a hundred.

e I'm sorry we couldn't *make* your party on Friday. We didn't get back until midnight.

f I'm having my hair *done* this afternoon.

F Verb-adverb collocations

1 Which adverbs in the box can follow these verbs? Make five lists.

drive   sleep   speak   walk   work

> carefully / carelessly / clearly / dangerously / fast / hard / heavily / lightly / loudly / noisily / quickly / slowly

2 Complete these sentences with verb-adverb collocations from **F1**.

a I can't hear what you're saying. Can you _____ more _____, please?

b We'll have to _____ a little more _____ if we want to get there on time.

c He was arrested for _____ _____. He admitted doing over 100 mph.

d You won't wake him. He always _____ _____.

e She's one of our best employees. She always _____ _____.

3 Someone who *eats noisily* is a *noisy eater*. What do we call these people?

a someone who *drives carefully* _____

b someone who *speaks clearly* _____

c someone who *sleeps lightly* _____

d someone who *works hard* _____

e someone who *walks slowly* _____

G Puzzle

Read the clues and complete the puzzle. All the answers are words from this unit.

a An adjective describing an area where people live
b Great anger
c American English for *rubbish*
d Extremely angry
e A hand movement
f The opposite of *carelessly*
g Extremely good
h Extremely surprising
i The American English spelling of *catalogue*
j American English for *mobile phone*
k The noun related to *irritated*

A Introduction

1 These words are from the article below. Try to match them with their meanings.

a	*assessment*	1	to connect or relate
b	*concentration*	2	to investigate, to look into
c	*evidence*	3	a test or measurement
d	*explore*	4	related to the human mind and its abilities
e	*imitation*	5	an idea which might explain facts
f	*associate*	6	the ability to focus your attention on something
g	*mental*	7	not real, a copy
h	*theory*	8	proof, information which makes us believe something

2 Check in a dictionary the meaning of any of these words you do not understand.

B Reading

1 Read the article and decide whether these statements are true (**T**) or false (**F**). Do not try to fill the gaps yet.

a	Two groups took part in the chewing gum experiments.	T / F
b	Gum chewers had a better long-term memory than the others.	T / F
c	The scientists understand clearly why chewing gum improves memory.	T / F
d	People's heart rate increases when they chew gum.	T / F
e	Chewing gum helps people to concentrate on their studies.	T / F

To chew or not to chew

Experiments suggest that chewing gum can assist the memory.

The habit of chewing gum is usually **(a)**_____ with young people, pop stars, and football managers. But researchers now believe that it's a habit which can improve your memory. Experiments carried out by Lucy Wilkinson and Dr Andrew Scholey, at the University of Northumbria, studied the positive effects of chewing gum on people's **(b)**_____ abilities.

A group of 75 adults was split into three groups: one group chewed sugar-free gum, a second group copied the process of chewing but without gum – **(c)**_____ chewing, and a third group did nothing. During the experiments, a computerised **(d)**_____ took place of the subjects' attention abilities, their long-term memory, and their working memory.

The results showed that chewing gum in a natural way improved people's abilities in a number of memory tests, compared with imitation chewing and not chewing at all. The gum chewers showed an improvement in immediate and long-term memory: their ability to remember words was 35% better than the two other groups.

Dr Scholey said the researchers did not know exactly why chewing gum improved these abilities, but they were **(e)**_____ a number of **(f)**_____.

He said: "We found that people who chewed gum had better memory for word lists and holding information. We think the improvement may be to do with having something in your mouth. We checked heart rate and found it increased during chewing."

There was no concrete **(g)**_____ from the experiments to support the idea that chewing gum improved **(h)**_____ while studying.

2 Now read the article again and fill each gap with the correct form of one of the words from **A1**

C Related words

1 Fill the gaps in this chart with words related to the words given. Sometimes there are two words in one group. (X = no useful word at this level.)

Noun	Verb	Adjective	Adverb
a assessment _____ *	_____	X	X
b concentration	_____	_____	X
c evidence	X	_____	_____
d _____ _____ *	explore	_____	X
e imitation _____ *	_____	_____	X
f _____	associate	X	X
g _____	X	mental	_____
h theory	X	_____	_____

* *These words refer to people.*

2 Fill the gaps in these sentences with words you have added to the chart.
   a Amundsen was a famous Norwegian _____ who reached the South Pole.
   b Children often _____ the behaviour of their older brothers or sisters.
   c Someone had _____ been smoking in the room.
   d I find it difficult to _____ on my work when other people are talking.
   e _____, we could win the lottery this week, but it's very unlikely.
   f After two 3-hour exams in one day, I was _____ exhausted.

D Adjective-noun collocations

1 The adjectives **a–e** are from the article. Match them with their opposites **1–5**.
   a *long-term*   1 artificial
   b *mental*   2 theoretical
   c *natural*   3 negative
   d *positive*   4 physical
   e *concrete*   5 short-term

2 Which adjectives in **D1** can be used with these nouns?

   ability / effects / evidence / light / memory

3 Complete these sentences using adjective-noun collocations from **D1** and **D2**.

a He seems to have a _____ _____ to get on with people.

b There is no _____ _____ that using mobile phones is harmful.

c Most people don't like rain, but it does have some _____ _____: like helping plants to grow.

d My grandmother can clearly remember her schooldays but her _____ _____ is very poor. She can't remember what she did yesterday.

e Our office has no windows, so we have to work in _____ _____.

EXTENSION: 'Memory' verbs

Apart from *remember*, there are a number of other verbs related to memory and remembering.

1 Match the verbs with their meanings.

a	*memorise*	1	make you remember something you have to do
b	*recall*	2	make you remember something similar
c	*recognise*	3	bring something back to your memory
d	*remind you **of** something*	4	learn by heart so that you can remember it exactly
e	*remind you **to do** something*	5	identify something or someone you have seen before

2 Choose the best verb in the these sentences.

a Haven't we met before? I'm sure I *remind / recognise* you from somewhere.

b I'm terrible at *memorising / recognising* telephone numbers.

c She *reminds / recalls* me of my sister. She's got the same laugh.

d I'm sorry, but I can't *recall / memorise* having a phone conversation with you.

e Could you *remind / remember* me to buy my dad a birthday present tomorrow?

E Phrasal verbs with *carry*

The article says that Lucy Wilkinson and Andrew Scholey **carried out** experiments. *Carry out* means *do* or *perform*. Here are some more phrasal verbs with *carry* and their meanings.

- *get carried away* — behave in a strange way because you are enthusiastic about something
- *carry something off* — succeed in doing something difficult
- *carry on* — continue
- *carry something through* — finish doing something planned

Now choose the best *carry* verb in these sentences.

a Scientists have been *carrying out / carrying on* tests to discover how the virus is spread.

b Politicians are determined to *carry away / carry through* their plan to improve schools.

c Sorry, I didn't mean to interrupt you. Please *carry off / carry on*.

d That was a fantastic performance. I know you were nervous, but you *carried it off / carried it on* brilliantly.

e I'd never seen such a fantastic selection of CDs! I got a bit *carried away / carried off* and spent all my money.

F Nouns + prepositions

*The gum chewers showed an improvement **in** long-term memory.*
Fill the gaps in these sentences with one of the prepositions from the box.

> between / for / in / into / on / to

a Last year politicians got a 10% increase _____ their salaries.

b Chewing gum has a definite effect _____ people's ability to remember words.

c I have no objection _____ your chewing gum if it helps you to study.

d We had a choice _____ going by taxi or catching a train.

e She seems to have lost all interest _____ her studies.

f Everyone knows about his financial dependence _____ his parents.

g Has anybody got an explanation _____ his absence?

h Researchers have been doing research _____ the connection _____ chewing gum and memory.

i They have been getting support _____ their research from the makers of chewing gum.

G Practice

Read this short article about someone's bad memory. Fill the gaps with words and phrases from sections **A–E** above.

I've got a terrible **(a)** _____ for detailed facts. For example, I often
(b) _____ people by their faces, but I find it completely impossible to
(c) _____ their names. My **(d)** _____ memory is particularly bad. I can
(e) _____ the names of all my school friends but be completely unable to
(f) _____ the name of someone I met yesterday! The problem is worse if
I'm tired, and getting plenty of sleep seems to bring about an **(g)** _____ in
the situation.
All this may be associated with my inability to **(h)** _____ on what I'm
doing. For example, if I'm trying to read a book or watch TV, every little noise
or movement disturbs me. My friends point out that it's a **(i)** _____ problem
rather than a physical one, and not very serious, but that doesn't really help.

Job stress in Sweden

A Introduction

1 These words and phrases are from the article below. Try to match them with their meanings.

a	*burned out*	1	a person with special knowledge or skill
b	*campaign*	2	something that happens to you
c	*casualty*	3	ill, unwell
d	*clinic*	4	to concentrate (on), to give your attention (to)
e	*experience*	5	achieving or producing a lot
f	*expert*	6	a person who suffers as a result of something bad
g	*focus on*	7	exhausted due to overwork over a long period
h	*high-pressure*	8	a series of planned activities intended to achieve an aim
i	*productive*	9	stressful, demanding
j	*sick*	10	a place where people go for specialist medical help

2 Check in a dictionary the meaning of any of these words you do not understand.

B Reading

Read the article and fill each gap with the correct form of a word or phrase from **A1**

My personality had gone

Rosie Goldsmith describes making a radio programme about the problems of stress in Sweden.

I thought I was well prepared to make a programme about stress among Sweden's young high-tech workers. But I was in for a shock. Many young Swedes are not only stressed, they're completely **(a)** _____. Change has happened so quickly in Sweden and young people are **(b)** _____ of that change.

First I met Torbjorn Levin – a tall Swede in his thirties who used to run his own advertising business and worked on average 50–70 hours a week. He burned out. He describes the **(c)** _____: 'I felt empty. My personality had gone.' Torbjorn stopped work, went to his parents' home and slept for three months. Today he is working again, but differently: 'I take it one day at a time. I question *why* I do things.'

Next I went to talk to one of the country's leading **(d)** _____ on stress, Professor Alexander Perski, who runs a burnout **(e)** _____. He says that Swedes are not used to **(f)** _____ work. There's a feeling that they're losing control over their own lives.

But stress doesn't just affect individuals – it also involves enormous costs to the country. This worries the Swedish Social Affairs Minister, Ingela Thalen. 'The government is investing more money in research and support, and there are education **(g)** _____. But in the end,' she says, 'people are responsible for their own health.'

My final visit was to meet an inspiring boss, Jurgen Lerjestad, who has come up with a brilliant new idea: you work only six hours a day. You then have time for a real life – at home with the kids and doing sports and other leisure activities. When you're at work, you **(h)** _____ work – no long phone calls to the boyfriend or the bank. His staff are never **(i)** _____, they are more **(j)** _____ and more enthusiastic, and very few of them leave the company. They earn a full salary, and their clients are happier too.

C Adjective-noun collocations

1 Which nouns in the box can follow these adjectives from the article? Make four lists.

brilliant enthusiastic inspiring leading

expert / idea / meeting / politician / teacher / worker

2 Complete these sentences using adjective-noun collocations from **C1**.
(You will have to change the form of some of the nouns.)

a He is one of the country's _____ _____ on climate change.
He's always being interviewed on television.

b I've just had a(n) _____ _____. Why don't we start our own business?

c I was never interested in maths, probably because I didn't have a very _____

_____.

d Bill Clinton was one of the world's _____ _____ in the 1990s.

e The firm has a lot of _____ _____. They are always keen to get to work.

D Related words

Fill the gaps in this chart with words related to the adjectives given. Sometimes there are two words in one group. (X = no useful word at this level.)

	Noun	Verb	Adjective	Adverb
a	_____	X	brilliant	_____
b	_____ _____ *	_____	enthusiastic	_____
c	_____	_____	inspiring	X
d	_____ *	_____	leading	X
e	_____ _____ _____ *	_____	productive	_____

* These words refer to people.

EXTENSION 1: *High- / Low-*

The compound adjectives *high-tech* and *high-pressure* are used in the article. Make adjectives using *high-* or *low-* with these words to complete the sentences **a–g**.

class / cost / fat / level / lying / risk / speed

a A car that can go very fast is a _____ car.

b When you want to lose weight, you eat _____ food.

c Dangerous sports like bungee jumping or mountaineering are _____ sports.

d If you haven't got much money, you live in _____ housing.

e Rich or famous people might stay in a _____ hotel.

f A meeting between important people, for example between presidents of the most powerful countries in the world, is a _____ meeting.

g Land which is near the sea is _____ land.

E Phrasal verbs with *out*

The article tells us that Torbjorn Levin **burned out**. Phrasal verbs with *out* often have the meaning of an activity ending completely. Use the correct form of these verbs to fill the gaps in the sentences.

blow out   die out   knock out   run out   sell out   tire out

a The car won't start. I think it may have _____ _____ of petrol.

b I need a lot of sleep. Staying up late at night _____ me _____.

c Mike Tyson _____ _____ his opponent in the first round of their fight.

d Many rare birds and animals are _____ _____ because of pollution.

e The wind was so strong that it _____ _____ the fire.

f The latest Madonna CD is incredibly popular. The shops _____ _____ of <u>it on the first day</u>.

EXTENSION 2

What other meanings can **out** have? Match the verbs with **out** in these sentences with meanings **1–4**.

a I don't feel like cooking tonight. Shall we *eat out*?

b We need to *set out* early if we want to arrive by midday.

c There isn't room for all those clothes. You'll have to *throw* some of them *out*.

d The teacher asked one of the students to *give out* the books.

1 remove, get rid of
2 go to a restaurant
3 distribute
4 start a journey

F Three-part phrasal verbs

The article says that Jurgen Lerjestad **came up with** a brilliant new idea. This means he *thought of* or *produced* an idea.

Match the three-part phrasal verbs in sentences **a–f** with meanings **1–6**.

> **Note**
> The three parts of these verbs almost always stay together. Example:
> *A Did he come up with that idea?* [Not *Did he come up that idea with?*]
> *B No, I came up with it.* [Not *I came up it with.*]

a I must *get down to* my geography essay today.

b She never buys a train ticket. I don't know how she *gets away with* it.

c I wish you'd stop *going on about* your rich relatives!

d Many young children *look up to* their teacher when they first start school.

e Our hotel was disappointing, but the wonderful weather *made up for* it.

f I can't *put up with* that noise any longer. Please turn your music down.

1 admire and respect
2 talk for a long time about something, in an annoying way
3 escape without criticism or punishment for something wrong you have done
4 provide something good to compensate for something bad
5 start making an effort to do something
6 tolerate, bear, endure

G Confusing words

Choose the correct word to complete each sentence.

a Stress can have a terrible *affect / effect* on some people.
b When he was at school, he hated doing scientific *experiences / experiments*.
c When I was 18, I left *home / house* and went to university.
d I can only sunbathe for half an hour – I've got very *sensible / sensitive* skin.
e Her ring looks expensive, but actually it's completely *priceless / worthless*.
f I don't mind being *alone / lonely* – I've always enjoyed my own company.

H Practice

Read this short news report about what a German company is doing to make its workers' lives easier. Fill the gaps with the correct form of words and phrases from the box. There are **two words** you do not need to use.

affect / come up with / effect / employees / enthusiasm / experiences / experiments / expert / idea / productive

German Town Promotes Sleeping on the Job

A German town has found that sleeping on the job, even for limited periods, can have the **(a)** _____ of making workers more **(b)** _____.

For two years, civil servants in the small town of Vechta near Hamburg have been allowed twenty minutes after lunch to nap* in their office chairs or to relax in other ways. In the beginning workers didn't think much of the **(c)** _____, but then they were happier and they started working with more **(d)** _____.

The town **(e)** _____ the scheme because it had too much work for too few **(f)** _____, and no money to take on new civil servants. A local health insurance company gave them courses in napping. **(g)** _____ carried out by the Institute of Sleep Research and Medicine in Regensburg found that 22 percent of the entire German population naps regularly. But according to an **(h)** _____ at the Institute, Juergen Zulley, only Vechta had put the idea of sleeping on the job into practice.

'Work and sleep are normally seen as opposites, and many firms don't want to admit that their employees sleep at work,' Zulley said.

* to nap = to sleep for a short time

A short history of frozen food

A Introduction

1 You are going to read an article about using ice to keep food fresh. Here are some words and phrases from the article.

> crammed / crystal / to defrost / to freeze / freezer / freezing / frozen / to keep / mushy / naturalist / to preserve / to stuff / to thaw out

a Underline the **seven** words and phrases which are connected in some way with **ice**.

b What do you notice about **five** of these words?

c Match the words connected with ice with these meanings:
1 a place to keep food very cold
2 a small shape with many sides, made of ice
3 to make something ice-cold and solid
4 to allow something which was ice-cold to return to its normal condition
5 in an ice-cold, solid condition
6 very cold

d Find other words in the box that mean:
1 filled with a lot of things pushed together
2 to fill something tightly
3 to prevent from going bad
4 a person who studies living things
5 soft and wet
6 to stay fresh

2 Check in a dictionary the meaning of any of these words you do not understand.

B Reading

1 Read the article and answer these questions. Do not try to fill the gaps yet.

a Who first used ice to keep fish fresh?
b Where did Clarence Birdseye discover the idea of keeping fish fresh by using ice?
c How and why is slow-frozen fish horrible?
d What was the 'Springfield Experiment'?

THANK YOU MR BIRDSEYE

The Chinese invent everything first. In the 15th century they used to fill their fishing boats with lumps of ice, so that the fish would still be fresh when it was brought to land. And in 1626, Francis Bacon, an Englishman who some people think may have written Shakespeare's plays, died of pneumonia which he caught while he was **(a)** _____ a dead chicken with snow to see if it would keep. But we have Clarence Birdseye to thank for modern **(b)** _____ food.

Clarence was a **(c)** _____ and wild man of the woods. He dropped out of university to become a trapper and to study wildlife for the American Government in the Canadian Arctic north. He spent the three long winters of 1910 to 1913 in a small wooden hut with Mrs Birdseye, lots of dead fish and a bathtub. To **(d)** ____ the fish, he filled the bath with them and packed ice round them.

At some point food obviously ran short, so he **(e)** _____ some of the fish and cooked it. He learned, from the local Eskimos, that the faster he **(f)** _____ the fish, the better it tasted later. Slow-frozen fish is **(g)** _____ and horrible because big ice **(h)** _____ form inside it and break up the flesh, but a fish caught in **(i)** _____ winds and laid flat on the ice as soon as it is caught tastes lovely. There are lots more ice crystals inside it, but they are microscopic in size.

Back in New York, Clarence invented a machine to flash-freeze packets of fish by squeezing them between two very cold steel plates, and started Birdseye Frozen Sea-foods Inc. On March 6 1930, in the 'Springfield Experiment', 26 different frozen foods were sold from a **(j)** _____ in a shop in Massachusetts.

Today, your home freezer, which is probably **(k)** _____ with piles and piles of delicious frozen meals just waiting to **(l)** _____ , is the result.

2 Now read the article again and fill each gap with the correct form of a word or phrase from **A1**.

C Verbs + prepositions

*In 1626, Francis Bacon stuffed a dead chicken **with** snow. He died **of** pneumonia.*
Fill the gaps in the sentences with one of these prepositions.

> for / from / in / of / on / with

a After a day's fishing, his hands and all his clothes *smelt* _____ fish.
b Clarence Birdseye *succeeded* _____ finding a way of freezing fish.
c He *filled* the bath _____ fish and ice.
d These days many people *rely* _____ frozen food for their everyday meals.
e The taste of frozen food *depends* _____ how quickly it was frozen.
f We have Clarence Birdseye to *thank* _____ inventing a machine which froze fish quickly.
g Now we *pay* less _____ frozen fish than _____ fresh fish. *(Same word twice.)*
h After three nights in sub-zero temperatures, he was *suffering* _____ severe frostbite.

D Near synonyms

1 Find **five** groups of **three** words from this list which are similar in meaning.

> appalling / appetising / awful / delicious / to fill / heaps / horrible / loads / microscopic / minute / to pack / piles / to stuff / tasty / tiny

2 Fill the gaps in these sentences with words from **D1** in the correct form. Usually three words are possible, but in one case only two are possible.

   a That was probably the worst film I've ever seen. It was absolutely _____.

   b When the stone hit the car, the windscreen smashed into thousands of _____ pieces.

   c We _____ so many clothes into our cases that we could hardly close them.

   d Everyone was very kind this year. I got _____ of presents for my birthday.

   e Everything on the menu sounds really _____.

EXTENSION: Word stress

The word *minute* has two meanings, depending on whether the stress is on the first syllable or the second syllable:
I'll be there in a 'minute.   When my daughter was born she had mi'nute fingers.

Here are some more words which can have different meanings, depending on where the stress is. Choose the correct alternative in each sentence.

   a I don't really want to change jobs. I'm quite '*content / con'tent* where I am.
   b It took them several days to cross the '*desert / de'sert* from north to south.
   c Would anyone '*object / ob'ject* if I smoked a cigarette in here?
   d You'll need a special '*permit / per'mit* to work here.
   e I wonder who's going to '*present / pre'sent* the prizes at the school this year?
   f Let's put the rubbish out. The '*refuse / re'fuse* collectors will be here soon.

E Materials

Mr and Mrs Birdseye lived in a small **wooden** hut for three years.
Clarence Birdseye's machine froze fish by squeezing it between two very cold **steel** plates.

> **Notes**
> Most words for materials have only one form: **Steel** plates / The plates are made of **steel**.
>
> But *wood* and *wool* have two forms: A **wooden** hut / The hut was made of **wood**.
>   A **woollen** jacket / This jacket is made of **wool**.

What are these objects made of? Match each picture with a word or words from the box on **page 35**.

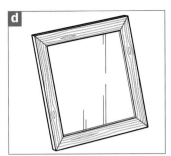

cloth (material) / glass / leather / metal / paper / plastic / pottery / rubber / wood

F Occupations

Clarence Birdseye was a *trapper* (someone who traps animals) and a *naturalist* (someone who studies living things).

Using one of the suffixes **-er / -ian / -ist / -or**, write the words used for someone who ...

a ... studies or plays *music* _____

b ... plays the *guitar* _____

c ... *cleans windows* _____

d ... *acts* in films _____

e ... studies *biology* _____

f ... has a job in *politics* _____

g ... studies *economics* _____

h ... *directs* a film or play _____

i ... *manages a company* _____

j ... *operates a computer* _____

G Puzzle

Find the following words in this puzzle. They can be horizontal, vertical or diagonal.

a Two 'ice' words
b Two words which mean *very small*
c Two words which mean *very bad*
d Two words with two different stress patterns for each
e Two different materials
f A theatrical occupation
g A musician

A	D	E	F	R	O	S	T	K	O
A	P	D	A	C	T	O	R	F	G
W	G	P	E	A	C	T	T	R	U
F	L	E	A	S	L	A	I	E	I
U	A	T	A	L	E	P	N	E	T
L	S	E	B	C	L	R	Y	Z	A
T	S	R	I	C	H	I	T	E	R
I	M	I	N	U	T	E	N	R	I
M	P	L	A	S	T	I	C	G	S
Y	O	C	O	N	T	E	N	T	T

Emails home

A Introduction

1 These words and phrases are from the two emails below. Try to match them with their meanings.

a	*area*	1	very busy
b	*backpacker*	2	a port, a place where ships stop to load and unload
c	*body clock*	3	wonderful
d	*cut costs*	4	a place where there is a natural spring of water which is good for drinking or bathing in
e	*harbour*	5	a geographical region, a part of a country
f	*hectic*	6	to reduce what you spend
g	*impressive*	7	a traveller who carries his/her possessions in a rucksack
h	*recover*	8	the human body's natural time to do certain things, e.g. sleep
i	*spa*	9	to return to a normal condition after tiredness or illness

2 These sets of words and phrases are also from the emails. Make up your own sentences using the words and phrases in each set in any order.
Example: *body clock / long flight   A long flight can affect / upset your body clock.*

a *hire / bike / explore / area*
b *beach / sand*
c *camp / sleeping bag / tent*

3 Check in a dictionary the meaning of any of the words in **A1** and **A2** you do not understand.

B Reading

Read the two emails and fill each gap with the correct form of a word or phrase from **A1** or **A2**.

Hi Dad,

We're safe and sound in Auckland, although totally exhausted. It's been a pretty **(a)** _____ few days exploring, finding our way around and **(b)** _____ from the longest flight you could imagine.

Auckland is quite **(c)** _____ – lots of good places to eat and stay and it's really quite hot! Our **(d)** _____ are still wrong. This morning we woke after 16 hours sleep at 5.30 a.m., wide awake and ready for a nice walk around the town and the **(e)** _____. We've decided to **(f)** _____ some bikes and then set about some proper exploration.

Anyway, as you can imagine, there's not a lot to tell you yet. We're just getting very hot and tired – all in the name of adventure.

I'll be checking my emails at least once a week so I should be able to keep up to date.

Hope all's well.

Lots of love,

Matthew xx

Hi!

How's it all going? We're back in Auckland after a week at Piahia, in a region called the Bay of Islands. It was fantastic – lots of harbours, bays and lovely beaches. We slowed right down and spent time just relaxing. It was a good place to have a break after the busy city.

Tomorrow we're going north-east to an area called the Coramandel. It's most amazing feature is a hot water beach – a kind of natural **(g)** _____ right on the sand! Sounds strange, doesn't it? We have now decided to camp with our new tent and sleeping bags and really **(h)** _____. It'll be cheaper and healthier than the special hostels for **(i)** _____.

I sent a few postcards out a week or so ago. Have they arrived yet? Anyway, I hope you are all well and happy.

Love to everyone,

Matt xx

C Verb-noun collocations

1 Which nouns and phrases in the box can follow these verbs?

cut   find   have

> _the answer to a question / a bath / bread / a break / breakfast / costs / a cure for a disease / dinner / a holiday / prices / a rest / a scene from a film / a shower / the solution to a problem / taxes / your way (somewhere)_

2 Fill the gaps in these conversations with verb-noun collocations from C1 in the correct form.

a A I've been working non-stop all morning.

 B Why don't you _____?

b A The video seems shorter than the film we saw at the cinema.

 B Yes, I think they've _____ several _____.

c A Do you think they'll ever _____ for cancer?

 B Of course. They're making progress all the time.

d A Why are you so late? Was there a lot of traffic?

 B No, I couldn't _____. In the end I had to ask someone.

e A Have you _____ this year?

 B Yes, we went to Italy for three weeks. The weather was fantastic.

f A Do you know when people first started drinking coffee?

 B No, I don't, but you could _____ in an encyclopedia or on the Internet.

g A Why have you started shopping at the old supermarket again?

 B Because they've _____ their _____.

EXTENSION 1: Idioms with *cut*

Match the **cut** idioms in these sentences with meanings 1–5

a I saw my best friend in town yesterday and she just *cut me dead*.
b The fire alarm went off just after lunch, so we had to *cut* our meeting *short*.
c The children were making a terrible noise until the teacher told them to *cut it out*.
d The builders had to *cut corners* to finish the house on time, but the owner made them do some of the work again.
e The headteacher phoned the boy's parents to tell them he had been *cutting lessons*.

1 do quickly and cheaply, but not properly
2 finish early
3 ignore someone completely
4 miss, be absent from
5 stop doing something

D Phrasal verbs with *set*

In his email Matt says: *We've decided to hire some bikes and then* **set about** *some proper exploration.* Here *set about* means *start doing something enthusiastically or seriously*.

These are some more phrasal verbs with *set* and their meanings.

- *set back*   delay, hold up
- *set down*   write / put into writing
- *set off / out*   leave or start on a journey
- *set up*   establish or start something

Now choose the best *set* verb in these sentences.

a Last year my brother *set down / set up* a new Internet company selling CDs.
b As soon as the hurricane was over, they *set about / set up* repairing the damage.
c We've got a long journey tomorrow. We'll have to *set about / set off* early.
d The bad weather *set back / set down* the road repair programme by two months.
e Write a letter to the director, *setting down / setting off* your ideas clearly.

E Adverbs meaning 'completely'

In the first email, the writer says he was **wide** awake at 5.30.
Here *wide* means *completely* or *totally*. We can also use the following words with certain adjectives to mean *completely* or *totally*.

> *dead / fast / flat / wide*

Fill the gap in each sentence with a word from the box.

a The children had such a tiring day that they were _____ *asleep* by 6 o'clock.

b He seemed to be asleep although his eyes were _____ *open*.

c I passed the exam first time. I found it _____ *easy*.

d Sorry I can't come out tonight. I'm _____ *broke*.

e We all wanted to hear the president's speech – so everyone was _____ *quiet*.

F Comparative adjectives

In the second email, Matt says *It'll be* **cheaper** *and* **healthier** *than the special hostels.*

Cheaper is the comparative form of *cheap*.
Healthier is the comparative form of *healthy*.

What are the comparative forms of these adjectives from the emails?

a *busy* _____

b *exhausted* _____

c *good* _____

d *happy* _____

e *hot* _____

f *impressive* _____

g *lovely* _____

h *new* _____

i *safe* _____

j *special* _____

k *strange* _____

l *tired* _____

G Practice

Read Matt's father's reply to the two emails. Fill each gap with a word or phrase from the box. There are **two** words or phrases you do not need to use.

amazing / area / beach / body clock / camp / exhausted / harbour / hectic / hire / sleeping bag / tent / wonderful

Hi Matt,

Thanks for your emails – I'm glad to hear everything's working out OK. Funny to think you're over the other side of the world, yet keeping in touch is so easy.

I'm glad you're enjoying New Zealand. It sounds like a(n) **(a)** _____ place, although it's not surprising that you were **(b)** _____ to start with. It will probably be several weeks before your **(c)** _____ gets back to normal again.

It's a good idea to **(d)** _____ bikes to explore the **(e)** _____. A few weeks hard cycling should get you back in shape! The sunshine will make a big difference, too.

Have you started to **(f)** _____ yet? If so, I hope you bought a warm **(g)** _____ – it can get bitterly cold at night in a **(h)** _____.

I expect you'll have been to Coramandel by now. The hot water **(i)** _____ sounds **(j)** _____. I can't quite imagine it. Send me a photo of it if you can. By the way, your postcard arrived yesterday. Thanks.

We're all okay. Take care.

Love, Dad

9 Rowing across the Atlantic

A Introduction

1 These words and phrases are from the article below. Try to match them with their meanings.

a	*complete*	1	to start to have or feel
b	*develop*	2	a feeling
c	*loneliness*	3	great unhappiness
d	*misery*	4	the way in which someone is welcomed
e	*phobia*	5	to move a boat through water using two oars (pieces of wood)
f	*pull out*	6	unhappiness because of being alone
g	*reception*	7	to decide not to continue
h	*row*	8	an extreme and unreasonable fear
i	*sensation*	9	good times and bad times
j	*ups and downs*	10	to finish

2 Check in a dictionary the meaning of any of these words you do not understand.

B Reading

Read the article and fill each gap with the correct form of a word or phrase from **A1**.

Debra carries on alone

27-year-old rower Debra Veal has **(a)** _____ a journey across the Atlantic alone. As she landed in Barbados to a warm **(b)** _____ from excited islanders she announced: "It's an amazing **(c)** _____."

Debra, a former physical education instructor from London, who now runs her own Internet company, was supposed to make the 3,000-mile trip with her 35-year-old husband Andrew, but after only two weeks, he **(d)** _____ a terrible **(e)** _____ about the ocean and had to abandon the trip. The couple had decided to make the trip, which started from the Canary Islands on 7 October, so they could spend 'quality time' together.

When Andrew **(f)** _____, Debra decided to carry on **(g)** _____ the 750kg Troika Transatlantic across the ocean alone, avoiding passing ships and sharks, and living on beef stew. She got up every day at 5.30 to row, resting when she needed to, as she made the crossing from Tenerife to Barbados.

When she was asked about the experience she replied: "It has been a really mixed journey with lots of **(h)** _____. Strong winds and heavy seas were real problems, and I had a very bad moment when I was nearly run down by a supertanker which passed me by a few hundred metres. I used to think the sharks would be a danger, but they were more interested in the fish under my boat than what was in it. The **(i)** _____ was the really hard part. But in many ways the ocean has been a fantasy world for me. I've heard no world news, so have no knowledge of the wars, death, **(j)** _____ and destruction that have no doubt been going on. In my world, there has only been peace and beauty."

C Related words

1 Fill the gaps in this chart with words related to the nouns from the article.
(X = no useful word at this level.)

Noun	Verb	Adjective	Adverb
a beauty	X	_____	_____
b destruction	_____	_____	_____
c instructor	_____	_____	X
d knowledge	_____	_____	_____
e loneliness	X	_____	X
f misery	X	_____	_____
g peace	X	_____	_____
h sensation	_____	_____	_____

2 Fill the gaps in these sentences with adjectives you have added to the chart.
Do not use any adjective more than once.

a We found our lessons very _____ – she was an excellent teacher.

b People who read a lot are often _____ about many subjects.

c Newspapers often have _____ stories on their front page to attract more readers.

d We escaped from the city and spent a _____ weekend in the country.

e Why are you looking so _____? Have you had some bad news?

f High winds are quite often very _____. They can blow trees and houses down.

g She could be a model – she has an absolutely _____ face.

h If you go out to work, you have contact with people. People who work from home are often _____.

D Adjective-noun collocations

1 Which nouns in the box can follow these adjectives from the article?

hard   heavy   strong

coffee / decision / disk / leader / luck / opinion / rain / smoker / taste
traffic / wind / work

2 Fill the gaps in these conversations with the correct form of one of the collocations from **D1**.

a A He gets through thirty or forty cigarettes a day.

   B Really? I didn't know he was such a _____ _____.

b A Don't you like dark chocolate?

   B No the _____ is too _____ for me.

c A That must have been a really _____ _____ to take?

   B Yes, it was – I was awake all night trying to make up my mind what to do.

d A I've failed my driving test again.

   B Oh no – that's really _____ _____!

e A Why were you late for work this morning?

   B The _____ was _____ than usual – probably because of the weather.

f A Why do you think the new president is so popular?

   B Because most people like a _____ _____.

EXTENSION: Adjectives ending in *-ed* and *-ing*

1 Choose the correct adjectives in these sentences.

   a Debra Veal was met in Barbados by *excited / exciting* islanders.
   b She told reporters it was an *amazed / amazing* sensation.

2 What can you say about the difference between the following adjectives?

   The students were all *bored*.
   It was a *boring* lesson.

3 Choose the best adjectives in these sentences.

   a Did you see that TV programme about earthquakes last night? It wasn't very *interested / interesting*.
   b You look very *relaxed / relaxing*. Did you have a good holiday?
   c It's been a *tired / tiring* week. I've had to work late every night.
   d My brother sings in the shower. It's his most *annoyed / annoying* habit.
   e The dull winter weather makes some people feel *depressed / depressing*.

E Phrasal verbs

Find these phrasal verbs in the article and notice how they are used. Then complete sentences a–e using the appropriate form of each verb.

carry on   get up   go on   pull out   run down

a Andrew _____ _____ of the trip when he found he was afraid of the sea.

b Debra was very brave to _____ _____ alone.

c She had to _____ _____ early every day and start rowing.

d The most dangerous moment was when a big ship almost _____ her _____.

e She didn't know what had been _____ _____ because she hadn't heard the news during her trip.

F Phrasal verbs with *pull*

1 Match these *pull* verbs with one or more of meanings a–g.

pull down   pull in   pull out   pull off   pull through

   a destroy (a building)
   b succeed in doing something difficult
   c withdraw from / stop doing something
   d stop by the side of the road (a car)
   e recover from a very serious illness
   f remove quickly (e.g. clothes)
   g leave the side of the road (a car)

2 Now complete these sentences with the appropriate form of *pull* verbs from **F1**.

a In last night's match, Manchester United _____ _____ one of their best wins ever.

b James was very ill after his operation, but he _____ _____.

c The apartment block they _____ _____ yesterday was only 20 years old.

d The champion had to _____ _____ of the race after he fell and injured his leg.

e We nearly had an accident when the bus _____ _____ in front of us.

G People

Match these words for people with the correct definitions.

a *instructor*
b *islander*
c *pedestrian*
d *resident*
e *motorist*
f *hooligan*
g *passer-by*
h *employee*
i *witness*
j *immigrant*

1 someone who comes to live permanently in another country
2 someone who works for a company or organisation
3 someone who sees an event take place and can describe it to others (e.g. a crime or accident)
4 someone who is noisy and violent in public
5 someone who teaches other people how to do something
6 someone who is walking, not driving a car or using public transport
7 someone who lives on an island
8 someone who lives in a place, not a visitor
9 someone who is going past a place (especially when an unusual event takes place)
10 someone who is driving a car

H Puzzle

Read the clues and complete the puzzle. All the answers are words from this unit.

a An extreme fear of something – e.g. insects, flying
b To damage something so badly that it no longer exists
c A computer has a _____ *disk* for storing information.
d The opposite of *war*
e Someone who is not a visitor but lives in a place

f The way in which someone is welcomed
g The opposite of *weak*
h Great unhappiness
i An adjective which describes a smoker who smokes a lot
j Fed up, irritated, a bit angry
k Someone who is walking, not using transport

k

a _ _ _ _ _ _
b _ _ _ _ _ _ _
c _ _ _ _
d _ _ _ _ _
e _ _ _ _ _ _ _
f _ _ _ _ _ _ _ _ _
g _ _ _ _ _
h _ _ _ _ _ _
i _ _ _ _ _
j _ _ _ _ _ _

A journey to remember

A Introduction

1 These words are from the article below. Try to match them with their meanings.

a confidently
b contrast
c deserted
d destroy
e found
f honk
g proudly
h purchase
i timidly
j tragically

1 empty of people
2 in a way which shows pleasure and satisfaction
3 very sadly
4 to use a car horn to make a noise
5 to buy
6 to ruin completely, to cause extreme damage to
7 not nervously, in a way which shows you believe you can do something
8 shyly and nervously
9 to establish, to begin
10 a clear difference

2 Check in a dictionary the meaning of any of these words you do not understand.

B Reading

Read the article and fill each gap with the appropriate form of a word from **A1**.

Arrival in Antigua

We flew into Guatemala City on a cool morning. Ours was the first flight of the day, so the airport was practically **(a)** _____. We knew we had to catch a bus to Antigua.

Uncertain what to do next, we walked **(b)** _____ out of the airport building. A strong-looking young man appeared.

"Taxi?"

We didn't know whether we needed a taxi, so we asked, "Bus station? Antigua? "

"Yes, taxi," he replied

(c) _____ and took us to an old blue Chevrolet.

Although there was little traffic on the roads, he **(d)** _____ frequently and drove as fast as he could. We reached the bus station in no time. As we were paying the driver, our bus started to pull away. We yelled desperately, and it slowed just enough for us to jump on.

About an hour-and-a-half later, we arrived in Antigua. It was still early morning and the air was cool. At the tourist office, we met a very friendly Antiguan who **(e)** _____ told us about his city. Antigua was **(f)** _____ in 1543 as the capital of Central America and the home of the Spanish colonial government. For more than 200 years, it was an important cultural and political centre. **(g)** _____, however, many of its beautiful old buildings had been **(h)** _____ in earthquakes in 1773 and 1976.

Of all the people we met that day, the children made a lasting impression on me because of the sharp **(i)** _____ with children at home. A common sight was young girls dressed in the famous orange, violet, red and indigo colours of Guatemala, carrying baskets filled with bright, hand-woven belts, coin purses and bracelets.

"You want to buy bracelet?" asked one particularly remarkable girl selling handmade goods. "Business not good today. You buy something?"

"Where did you learn to speak English so fluently?" I asked. "In school?"

"No, I don't go to school."

"Did you learn by talking to customers?" I asked.

She nodded. We **(j)** _____ a couple of coin purses, which made her very happy.

C Related words

1 Complete this chart with words related to the adverbs from the article.
(X = no useful word at this level.)

Adverb	Adjective	Noun
a confidently	_____	_____
b desperately	_____	_____
c fluently	_____	_____
d frequently	_____	_____
e particularly	_____	X
f proudly	_____	_____
g timidly	_____	_____
h tragically	_____	_____

2 Fill the gaps in these sentences with adjectives or nouns you have added to the chart.

a Some athletes are so _____ to win that they take dangerous drugs.

b It's a _____ that she died so young. She had her whole life to look forward to.

c It was simply his _____ that prevented him from answering the teacher's question. He's very intelligent, but he lacks self- _____.

d Is there a _____ reason why you want to meet him? Or is it just out of interest?

e If you are bilingual, it means you are _____ in two languages.

f She's a _____ visitor to this country. She comes five or six times a year.

g Her parents are very _____ of her achievements. They are always telling everyone how clever she is.

D Adjective-noun collocations

1 Which nouns in the box can follow these adjectives from the article? One noun goes with two different adjectives.

common   lasting   sharp

> *bend (in the road) / contrast / effect / flower / impression / increase / knife / name / relationship / sight / teeth*

2 Which collocations from **D1** could be used to refer to the following?

  a a rose or a daisy
  b a friendship which continues for many years
  c John or Anne
  d somewhere you ought to drive very carefully

EXTENSION 1: Verbs ending in -en

If you want to make a pencil *sharp*, you *sharpen* it. Make verbs ending in -en from the adjectives in the box, then use them to complete the sentences.

loose / short / straight / sweet / tight / wide

a Your trousers are too long. You should _____ them.

b That picture looks crooked. Shall I _____ it for you?

c This road is dangerously narrow. They should _____ it.

d My bicycle wheel was coming loose so I had to _____ it.

e People put sugar in their coffee to _____ it.

f He can't breathe! _____ his tie!

Note If you want to make something *longer*, you *lengthen* it.
If you want to make something *stronger*, you *strengthen* it.

E Verb-noun collocations

1 Which nouns in the box can follow these travel verbs and phrases? (Some nouns can follow more than one verb.)

catch   drive   miss   ride   travel by

bicycle / boat / bus / car / coach / horse / motorbike / plane / taxi / train

2 Find the best endings for these sentence beginnings, and fill each gap with the correct form of one of the verbs or phrases from **E1**.

Beginnings	Endings
a Sorry I can't stop – I'm in a hurry ...	1 I learnt to _____ a bike when I was three.
b She's frightened of flying ...	
c I've always been a keen cyclist –	2 as soon as they are 17 years old.
d When I go to work ...	3 so she's going to _____ boat.
e Many British people learn to _____ a car ...	4 because I'm frightened of animals.
	5 because I don't want to _____ my bus.
f I've never learnt to _____ a horse ...	6 I usually _____ the 6.45 train.

EXTENSION 2: Expressions with *catch*

Replace *catch* or *caught* in each sentence with the correct form of a verb from the box.

attract / capture / find / get / hear

a While he was on holiday he *caught* flu and was in bed for several days.

b I've been trying to *catch* the waiter's attention for ten minutes already.

c The police *caught* the criminals as they made their getaway.

d Can you say that again? I didn't quite *catch* what you said.

e It was so embarrassing – my friend *caught* me reading her private diary.

F Travel nouns

Complete the table with nouns from the box. You will need to use one noun twice.

> bus / bus station / driver / pilot / plane / port / sailor / railway station

Place	Vehicle	Person
a airport	_____	_____
b _____	boat	_____
c _____	_____	driver
d _____	train	_____

G Compound adjectives

1 The girls were selling **hand-woven** belts, purses and bracelets.
Match these compound adjectives with the correct descriptions of how they are formed.

> curly-haired / fast-moving / handmade / hand-woven / long-legged / strong-looking

a noun + past participle
b adjective + -ing word
c adjective + noun + -ed

2 Which compound adjectives could be used to describe the following?

a a business which is financed by the government   _____

b something which is shaped like an egg   _____

c someone who has a warm heart   _____

d a film in which the action moves very slowly   _____

e a flower which smells sweet   _____

f someone who writes with their left hand   _____

H Practice

Read this short article about a journey and fill each gap with a word from the box.

> attention / catch / deserted / driver / fluently / long / missed / railway / timidly / train

I was alone in a strange country. I knew a bit of the language, but I couldn't speak it **(a)** _____. I had arrived at the **(b)** _____ station two minutes late and had **(c)** _____ the last **(d)** _____. I stood there on the **(e)** _____ platform, wondering what to do. Perhaps I could **(f)** _____ a bus back into town and stay in a hotel. As I left the station a **(g)** _____-haired man waved to attract my **(h)** _____. "Taxi?" he said. Before I could answer, he took my case and put it into his car. "How much?" I asked **(i)** _____. I was worried because I didn't have much money. "Tonight my taxi is free," announced the taxi **(j)** _____. "I've just won the lottery!"

Claiming compensation

11

A Introduction

1 These words and phrases are from the article below. Try to match them with their meanings.

a	*blame*	**1**	money paid to make up for injury or inconvenience
b	*fault*	**2**	connected with the law
c	*claim*	**3**	money paid for professional services, e.g. to a lawyer
d	*compensation*	**4**	physical harm or damage
e	*be entitled to*	**5**	to say someone or something is responsible for something bad
f	*fees*	**6**	a hard path for walking on at the side of a road
g	*injury*	**7**	an increase
h	*legal*	**8**	responsibility for something bad
i	*pavement*	**9**	to have a right to something
j	*rise*	**10**	a demand for money you think you have a right to

2 Check in a dictionary the meaning of any of these words you do not understand.

B Reading

1 Read the article and fill each gap with the correct form of a word or phrase from **A1**.

Oy! Watch out where you're going!

Whose fault is it?

An advertisement in Britain tells the public: "If you have been injured while playing a sport, you may **(a)** _____ a large sum of money in compensation." The advert also promises **(b)** _____ assistance in obtaining compensation for accidents at work, for car crashes and for other **(c)** _____. One company which provides this legal service says that it receives 30,000 requests for help every month. Some companies guarantee that if they lose a compensation **(d)** _____, the customer will not have to pay them any **(e)** _____.

Local councils are having to pay out larger and larger amounts of compensation in a wide range of cases – for example, to people who have fallen in towns and are (f) _____ the bad condition of (g) _____ , or to parents who blame a school because their children have failed their exams. The head of an insurance company which deals with some of these cases says "More and more people believe that when things go wrong, it must be someone's (h) _____ . If you can find someone to blame, you claim (i) _____ . People don't want to take responsibility for anything these days. If you walk into a wall, it's the wall's fault for being there. Many people think of this as an easy way of making money."

Doctors, dentists and social workers are also being blamed for things that go wrong in people's lives, and this is costing the country billions of pounds every year. Does this really mean that Britain is becoming more like America, where people go to court first and ask questions later? And if there is a sudden (j) _____ in compensation claims, who will end up paying? As usual, it will be ordinary members of the public or the customers of insurance companies who will lose.

2 Answer these questions about the article, using appropriate phrases from the box.

> blame the school / claim compensation / insurance companies / legal assistance / lose their claim / make money

a What may people injured in car crashes be able to do?
b What are the companies who advertise offering?
c In what situation do customers not have to pay legal fees?
d What do some parents do if their children fail exams?
e Why do so many people make compensation claims?
f Who usually pays the money in compensation claims?

C Verb-noun collocations

1 Which nouns in the box can follow these verbs from the article?

make   pay   take

> advice / care / an exam / fees / fun of someone / a joke / medicine / money / notes / a photo / a profit / rent / responsibility (for) / tax(es)

2 Complete these sentences using collocations from **C1**.

a There's no point in suggesting anything to him – he never _____ _____ .
b The doctor gave me two different kinds of _____ to _____ .
c In their first year of business the company _____ a small _____ .
d Don't _____ _____ of him – even if you don't mean it. He just can't _____ a _____ .
e If you own your house, you don't have to _____ _____ .
f _____ _____ when you cross the road – the traffic is very busy at this time of day.

D Expressions with *go* + adjective

In the article, the head of the insurance company says *People believe that when things* **go wrong**, *it must be someone's fault.* When something *goes wrong*, it doesn't happen in the way it should. For questions **a–h**, choose the appropriate answers **1–8**.

a What should you do if someone *goes missing*?

b Why do people *go red*?

c What happens if someone *goes blind*?

d When does food *go bad*?

e What happens if someone *goes bald*?

f When do people *go grey*?

g Why do people *go berserk*?

h What happens if someone *goes quiet*?

1 Because they feel very angry, and can't control themselves.

2 They can't see.

3 When they are old.

4 Look for them and then contact the police.

5 When it is old and no longer fresh.

6 They stop talking.

7 Because they are embarrassed.

8 They lose their hair.

EXTENSION 1: Colour expressions

Choose the correct colour from the box to complete each sentence. Be careful – there is one extra colour!

black / blue / green / red / white / yellow

a When Paul asked Jackie to marry him, she didn't know what to say – the question came completely out of the _____.

b My brother's just bought a fantastic new car. As you can imagine, I'm absolutely _____ with envy.

c I'll only believe they are giving me the job when I see something in _____ and _____.

d I had a shock this morning. A letter from the bank said I'm over £1000 in the _____! I don't know how I'm going to pay it back.

e "How would you like your coffee?" "_____ please, but not too much milk."

E *Blame* and *fault*

1 Look at these examples of sentences using *blame* or *fault*.

She says it's his fault. = She blames him.
They said everything was my fault. = They blamed me for everything.

2 Rewrite these sentences using *blame* or *fault*.

a I think the accident was John's fault.

b They blamed the government for the disaster.

c Don't say it's my fault.

d I blame Rachel.

F Formal and informal words

Match the formal words **a–f** from the article with the informal equivalents **1–5**.

a	*assistance*	**1**	get
b	*guarantee*	**2**	give
c	*injured*	**3**	help
d	*obtain*	**4**	hurt
e	*provide*	**5**	promise
f	*receive*		

EXTENSION 2: Meanings of *get*

The verb *get* has many meanings. Which of the meanings in the box does *get* have in sentences **a–f**?

> *arrive / become / buy / earn / receive / understand*

a I'm going into town to *get* some new jeans.
b Sorry, I don't *get* what you mean. Can you tell me again, please?
c Can we go home now? I'm *getting* really tired.
d My sister *got* a CD player for her 18th birthday.
e If we *get* there early, we'll have time for a coffee.
f Dave's fairly well-off – he *gets* over £30,000 in his new job.

G Puzzle

Find the following words in this puzzle. They can be horizontal, vertical or diagonal.

a Two formal words meaning *get*
b A formal word meaning *help*
c A formal word meaning *hurt*
d Two nouns which can follow *make*
e Two nouns which can follow *take*
f Two adjectives which can follow *go*
g A colour connected with envy
h A colour connected with owing money

A	R	P	R	O	F	I	T	E	P
A	S	T	I	L	M	E	G	T	J
W	G	S	I	B	A	L	D	Y	O
L	L	E	I	N	K	E	R	C	K
I	R	E	D	S	J	S	Q	A	E
V	S	E	B	C	T	U	R	U	I
I	S	E	A	R	N	A	R	U	W
N	A	D	V	I	C	E	N	E	L
G	G	R	E	Y	D	T	C	C	D
G	R	E	E	N	E	B	U	Y	E

A Introduction

1 These words and phrases are from the article below. Try to match them with their meanings.

a	*alternative*	1	to make, to get ready
b	*consist of*	2	a worker trained in special scientific skills
c	*cosmetics*	3	one part of the contents of something (e.g. a cooking recipe)
d	*discovery*	4	something that can be used instead of something else
e	*equivalent to*	5	something added to something else to improve it
f	*impress*	6	something you find out
g	*ingredient*	7	different kinds of make-up
h	*prepare*	8	to be made up of, to include
i	*supplement*	9	to have a favourable effect on, to influence positively
j	*technician*	10	having the same value as

2 Check in a dictionary the meaning of any of these words and phrases you do not understand.

B Reading

Read these three short news stories and fill each gap with the correct form of a word or phrase from **A1**.

Odd News Odd News Odd News Odd News

Raspberries help you slim

A Japanese cosmetics company has brought out a slimming pill that uses the power of raspberries to burn unwanted fat. The pleasant-tasting pill has really **(a)** _____ Japanese women who are trying to lose weight.

Each pill is loaded with raspberry ketones, the **(b)** _____ which reduces fat, and is **(c)** _____ to 1,000 fresh raspberries. The **(d)** _____ company claims that 70 per cent of people who took part in a study of the raspberry **(e)** _____ each lost an average of one kilo after taking the pills for a week.

The company also produces an **(f)** _____ to the pills which has the same effect: 'sheets' containing raspberry ketones that can be placed on parts of the body.

The Viennese Vegetable Orchestra

Forget the cello, just listen to that 'cucumberophone'! The First Viennese Vegetable Orchestra, which **(g)** _____ of eight musicians, a sound **(h)** _____ and a cook, plays vegetable instruments they make themselves. Their instruments can produce sounds that cannot easily be made by a normal orchestra. It takes the band about half an hour to make a carrot flute, and under 15 minutes to make a 'cucumberophone'. Other instruments include aubergine cymbals and pumpkin drums.

At the end of a performance, the stage is cleared and the cook uses the instruments to **(i)** _____ a soup for the audience and the musicians. The audience can once again enjoy what they have just heard. 'We employ a real chef,' says the band, 'so the soup is tasty and very special.'

Chocolate is good for you

American scientists have discovered that a group of chemicals found in cocoa beans, from which chocolate is made, can increase the production of nitric oxide, which helps to keep our blood pressure at a safe level. The highest levels of these chemicals are found in cocoa drinks, but are also present in dark, and even milk, chocolate.

Professor Norman Hollenberg, who led the study, said: 'Nitric oxide is very necessary for healthy blood pressure and therefore for keeping the heart in good condition. This **(j)** _____ could be of great importance for public health.'

C Related words

1 Fill the gaps in this chart with words related to the words given. (X = no useful word at this level.)

Noun	Verb	Adjective	Adverb
a _____	discover	X	X
b importance	X	_____	_____
c _____	include	_____	X
d _____	X	necessary	_____
e supplement	_____	_____	X
f _____	prepare	_____	X
g _____	reduce	X	X
h _____	X	safe	_____

2 Fill the gaps in these sentences with words you have added to the chart.

a There used to be accidents at work every day. Now _____ is taken more seriously.

b This meal doesn't need a lot of _____ – it'll be ready in about 20 minutes.

c Motorists are delighted about this week's _____ in the price of petrol.

d You must vote tomorrow. It's the most _____ election for 20 years.

e Many people take vitamins to _____ their diet.

f A television isn't a _____, you know! You don't actually need one!

D Adjective-noun collocations

1 Which nouns in the box can follow these adjectives? One noun goes with two different adjectives.

general   normal   public

behaviour / day / election / health / holiday / interest / knowledge / opinion / price / relations / rule / way

2 Which collocations from **D1** mean the following?

a what you usually pay for something
b the occasion when people vote for a new national government
c how most people do something
d what ordinary people think about a subject
e non-specialised information which people have about all kinds of subjects
f a day on which most people in a particular country don't go to work

E Nationalities

Which countries do the three news stories relate to? Write them in the correct spaces in the chart. Then complete the rest of the chart.

Country	Nationality
a _____ (Story 1)	_____
b _____ (Story 2)	_____
c _____ (Story 3)	_____
d China	_____
e Egypt	_____
f _____	Canadian
g Sweden	_____
h _____	Spanish
i The Netherlands	_____
j Iraq	_____
k _____	Thai

F Adjectives + prepositions

*Each pill is loaded **with** raspberry ketones.*
Complete each sentence below with one of the prepositions from the box.

> *about / at / for / of / to*

a Unfortunately he doesn't have the qualifications necessary _____ the job.

b Five British pounds is equivalent _____ about eight Euros.

c Thanks a lot. I'm very grateful _____ the offer.

d Are you available _____ work? If so, you can start on Monday.

e Have you got any good ideas? I'm quite open _____ suggestions.

f Where have you been? I've been so worried _____ you!

g Children are sometimes afraid _____ the dark.

h I am completely opposed _____ the plan to build a new airport near here.

i Fruit and vegetables are good _____ you.

j Julie has always been good _____ languages.

EXTENSION: Adjectives starting with a...

Many English adjectives starting with *a...* cannot be used immediately before a noun. For example, it is not correct to say: [*the afraid child*]. We say: *The child is afraid* or *the frightened child*.

Make phrases from these sentences using another adjective before each noun.

a The passengers are *asleep.* _____

b The car is *ablaze.* _____

c The creatures are *alive.* _____

d The ship is *afloat.* _____

G Homophones

A homophone is a word which sounds like another word, but has a different spelling and meaning. For example, *no* and *know* are homophones.

Here are some words from the news stories. Can you think of a homophone for each word using the clues?

		Homophone	Clue
a	*weight*	_____	to stay where you are until someone comes
b	*week*	_____	the opposite of *strong*
c	*hour*	_____	belonging to us
d	*cymbal*	_____	a sign or object which represents something else
e	*led*	_____	a heavy metal / the part of a pencil which writes
f	*so*	_____	to make or repair using a needle and thread

H Puzzle

Read the clues and complete the puzzle. All the answers are words from this unit.

a To be made up of = *to _____ of.*
b Usual, ordinary
c Thankful
d Act, show, entertainment
e Burning
f Someone from the Netherlands is this.
g Someone skilled in practical science
h Decrease (noun)
i A new government is voted for in this kind of election.
j Things like *lipstick* and *mascara*, used to improve your appearance
k Something that is used in cooking

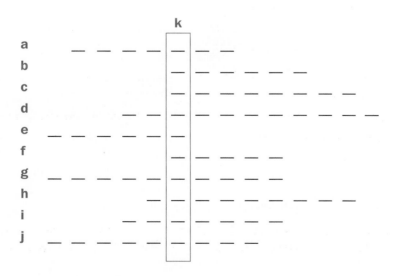

A Introduction

1 These words are from the article below. Try to match them with their meanings.

a	*agriculture*	1	strength, power
b	*cage*	2	to teach, to instruct
c	*force*	3	to look at for a long time
d	*herd*	4	farming, the farming business
e	*pet*	5	to gather animals together
f	*stare*	6	an animal kept at home for pleasure
g	*stubborn*	7	to move away from a place
h	*tough*	8	a place where animals and birds are kept, often made of wire
i	*train*	9	obstinate, refusing to change your mind
j	*wander*	10	strong, hard-working

2 Check in a dictionary the meaning of any of these words you do not understand.

B Reading

1 Read the article and fill each gap with the correct form of a word from **A1**. You will need to use one of the words twice.

The shepherd's best friend

When Bob Hooker was a student in Texas, he came across something that astonished him. He was keeping horses at the home of a man who **(a)** _____ border collies.

"The first day I went there, I noticed he had some puppies in a **(b)** _____," says Hooker. "One made a hole in the side and got into an area with chickens. The puppy went around the chickens, gathering them up in the centre, then lay down and watched them. When they started to **(c)** _____ from the centre, he patiently rounded them up again. He did that over and over again. I was amazed." Hooker decided then and there that he wanted to find out more about these dogs and to have one himself. So he went to Britain, the original home of

the border collie. Here he found world-class trainers, learned more and bought dogs from them. Now, at the age of 56, he is a trainer himself.

"If you're in **(d)** _____, every animal you own should be able to make money for you," he says. "So, certainly, you can have a dog as a **(e)** _____, but all the better if it can **(f)** _____ animals. But you must have one which is right for the purpose, and there's none better than the border collie. It's a **(g)** _____ dog that can do the work of twenty people."

The border collie lives to work and is ideal with sheep. It doesn't move the animals by

(h) _____, but by the power of its presence and by **(i)** _____ at them intently. Occasionally a **(j)** _____ animal has to be shown who's boss, but the dog works silently, able to work out different situations. It is intelligent, quick, easy to **(k)** _____ and hard-working. In fact, it's unhappy if it's not working, which makes it a good partner for farmers with animals, but not such a good pet, unless you can keep it busy.

2 How much do you remember about the article? Answer these questions, then read the article again to check your answers.

   a Where did Bob Hooker first see border collies?
   b What did the puppy do which surprised Bob Hooker?
   c Where did he go to find out more about border collies?
   d What does Bob Hooker do now?
   e Why don't border collies make good pets?

C Animals

1 Group the animal words in the box under the headings below. Some animals can belong to more than one group. One example of each is given.

> camel / cat / chicken / cow / deer / dog / donkey / duck / elephant / giraffe / horse / lion / monkey / pig / rabbit / sheep / tiger / turkey

Pets	Working animals	Farm animals and birds	Wild animals and birds
rabbit	dog	chicken	giraffe

2 Add any more animals and birds you know to the four groups.

3 Match these animals with their young.

   a cat   **1** cub
   b cow   **2** foal
   c dog   **3** piglet
   d horse   **4** kitten
   e lion   **5** lamb
   f pig   **6** calf
   g sheep   **7** puppy

EXTENSION: Animal idioms

What could you call the people below? Choose the correct idiom from the box.

a Someone who shows no feelings or emotions
b Someone we don't know much about – perhaps they have a secret life
c Someone who gets up at 5 o'clock in the morning and starts work before everyone else
d Someone who is always active, who never stops doing things
e Someone who is used in an experiment, for example to test a new kind of medicine
f Someone who is very important or powerful in an organisation, like a government minister or a managing director

> *an early bird / the top dog / a cold fish / a dark horse / a busy bee / a guinea pig*

D Phrasal verbs

1 Match these phrasal verbs from the article with one or more of meanings a–f.

come across   find out   lie down   round up   work out

a gather together
b calculate the answer to a problem, understand something
c find, see or meet by chance
d put yourself into a horizontal position, to rest or sleep
e do physical exercise to make yourself fit
f learn, discover

2 Complete each sentence with the correct form of one of the phrasal verbs from **D1**.

a You're looking incredibly fit. Have you been _____ _____?

b I _____ _____ everything I know about animals from working on a farm in my holidays.

c The children had spent all day on the beach. Eventually their parents _____ them _____ and took them home.

d You look exhausted. You should go and _____ _____.

e While I was tidying the cellar, I _____ _____ a collection of old family photos.

f Can I borrow your calculator? I can't _____ _____ what 25 per cent of £3.50 is.

E Phrasal verbs with *come*

Choose the correct phrasal verb in each of these sentences.

a When we were trying to repair the car, we *came out with / came up against* all kinds of problems.
b A fantastic job has *come up / come round* in London. It's ideal for me so I'm going to apply for it.
c Did you watch the interview with the princess? She *came out with / came up with* some amazing bits of gossip.
d When she *came round / came by* she was in bed holding her baby. Everyone was smiling and congratulating her.
e *Come off / Come on*! If you don't hurry up, we'll be late.
f I'm living in New York now, but I actually *come by / come out of / come from* Scotland.

F 'Seeing' verbs

Complete the sentences with the correct form of one of these 'seeing' verbs. Sometimes more than one answer is possible.

> gaze at / look at / notice / see / stare at / watch

a Did you _____ the late film on TV last night?

b I can't _____ properly – I think I need to have my eyes tested.

c Why are you _____ me like that?

d It was their first romantic meal together. They spent the whole evening _____ each other.

e 'Did you _____ the colour of the car she was driving?' 'I'm not sure. I think it was green.'

f _____ that girl over there! She looks exactly like someone I was at school with.

G Puzzle

Read the clues and complete the puzzle. All the answers are words from this unit.

a A kind of horse we don't know much about
b A verb which can mean to look at someone romantically
c Another word for *instructor* or *teacher*
d A *cold* _____ is someone who has no feelings.
e A young lion
f Another word for *obstinate* – like a donkey
g A young cow
h A young cat
i A young dog
j To look at hard without turning your eyes away
k Animals and birds are kept in this in a zoo.
l The business of farming

A Introduction

1 These words are from the article below. Try to match them with their meanings.

a	*convinced*	**1**	difficult or impossible to believe
b	*flabbergasted*	**2**	a view of something for a very short time
c	*funnel*	**3**	to show, to make visible
d	*glimpse*	**4**	an image of something which is not really there
e	*incredible*	**5**	extremely surprised, amazed
f	*invert*	**6**	sure, certain
g	*mirage*	**7**	to turn upside down
h	*reveal*	**8**	a metal chimney

2 Choose the correct geographical word or phrase from the box for each label **a–f**

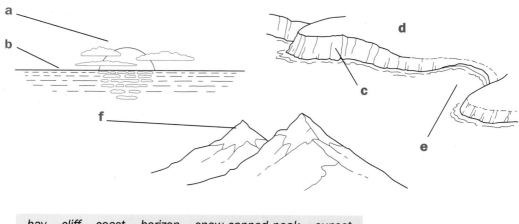

| bay | cliff | coast | horizon | snow-capped peak | sunset |

3 Check in a dictionary the meaning of any of these words you do not understand.

B Reading

1 Read the article and fill each gap with the correct form of a word or phrase from **A1** or **A2**

Village in the sky

There are no mountains or trains in the Orkney Islands of Scotland. So when the people of Sanday woke up one day to find that snow-capped peaks and a village with a train had appeared at the north end of their tiny island, they were **(a)** _____. They hadn't been there the day before. Yet suddenly there was a large white building with several smaller houses grouped around it. And the ghost village remained on view for several hours before vanishing at **(b)** _____. The islanders were **(c)** _____ that a trick of the light had brought them a **(d)** _____ of Norway, 800 kilometres away. Experts agreed that it was a mirage.

Another **(e)** _____ sight hung in the sky over Hastings on the south coast of England in July 1797. The **(f)** _____ of France suddenly appeared, clear as daylight, as if it was just across a **(g)** _____. Local resident William Latham wrote: "The coast of France could be clearly seen without a telescope. I could see **(h)** _____ on the opposite coast 50 miles distant." Sailors and fishermen could make out places they had visited, and with a telescope they could even see the French fishing boats.

(i) _____ like these are caused by the weather. When conditions are calm, and warm air sits on top of cool air, it creates what is called a *temperature inversion*. The place where the two types of air meet behaves like a mirror, creating amazing images and revealing places hidden under the curve of the earth.

Sometimes the temperature inversions actually **(j)** _____ the images as well. This happened in 1957 when passengers on the ship *Edinburgh Castle*, which was sailing up the English Channel, suddenly saw a line of ships on the **(k)** _____ – upside down, some on top of each other, funnel to funnel.

2 Match each sentence beginning with the correct ending. You may need to check your ideas in the article.

Beginnings	Endings
a The people of Sanday saw mountain peaks ...	1 if they used a telescope.
b The islanders thought ...	2 the coast of France.
c In 1797 the people of Hastings clearly saw ...	3 which were covered in snow.
d They could see fishing boats ...	4 looked as if they were upside down.
e The ships which the passengers on the *Edinburgh Castle* saw ...	5 they had seen a village in Norway.

C People

Find words in the article which mean the following. Someone who ...

a ... goes to sea to catch fish _____

b ... knows a lot about a particular subject _____

c ... lives permanently in a particular place _____

d ... lives on an island _____

e ... travels on a ship, a train or a plane _____

f ... works at sea _____

EXTENSION: More people

Think of words which mean the following. Someone who ...

a ... lives in a village _____

b ... travels by bicycle _____

c ... works in a shop _____

d ... buys things in a shop _____

e ... suffers as a result of a crime _____

f ... works in a library _____

g ... breaks the law _____

h ... works in a garden _____

i ... paints people's houses _____

j ... bets money on the lottery, horse-racing, etc _____

D Near synonyms

1 Find **six** groups of **three** words or phrases from the box which have similar meanings.

> a few / appear / become visible / calm / cause / clear / come into view / create /
> disappear / fade / on view / peaceful / produce / quiet / several / some / vanish / visible

2 Fill the gaps in these sentences with appropriate words and phrases from **D1**
Sometimes more than one word or phrase can be used.

a It is more comfortable to travel by ship when weather conditions are _____.

b When there are no clouds at night, the moon and stars are _____.

c Unusual weather conditions sometimes _____ strange mirages.

d These mirages sometimes last for _____ hours.

e We had been sailing for three hours, when suddenly the fog cleared and the coast
of France _____.

f The speedboat roared past us and in a few minutes had _____ over the horizon.

E Phrasal verbs with *make*

1 Choose the best meaning for *make out* in this extract from the article:
*Sailors and fishermen could **make out** places they had visited.*

a describe
b manage to see
c make contact with

2 Match these *make* verbs with one or more of the meanings below.

make for   make off   make up

a become friends again after an argument
b produce or invent something from your imagination, e.g. a recipe, a story, an excuse
c go in the direction of (a place)
d leave (a place) quickly

3 Complete these sentences with the correct form of one of the verbs from **E2**.

a I never use books when I'm cooking. I prefer to _____ _____ my own recipes.

b The thieves stole £3 million pounds worth of jewels from the shop and _____ _____ in a stolen car.

c They didn't speak to each other for a year after their row, but they eventually _____ _____ and have been the best of friends ever since.

d We set off at seven o'clock and _____ _____ the airport.

e I didn't believe a word of his story. It was obvious he was _____ it all _____ .

F Place prepositions

Fill the gaps in these sentences with suitable prepositions. There are similar sentences in the article.

a Felixstowe is a port _____ the east coast of England.

b The ship sailed _____ the river as far as the capital city.

c There were clouds in the sky _____ London all day long.

d There are lots of trees growing _____ our house.

e It was a clear day so we could easily make out four ships _____ the horizon.

f My grandparents live _____ the south end of the island.

G Puzzle

Find the following words in this puzzle. They can be horizontal, vertical or diagonal.

a Three adjectives which mean *believing strongly that something is true*
b Something you think you can see, but that doesn't actually exist
c The time in the evening when the sun disappears
d Very high rocks on the coast
e The line between the sky and the land or sea
f A very knowledgeable person
g An adjective describing something which it is possible to see
h Two adjectives which mean the same as *peaceful*

V	E	S	U	R	E	O	N	E	M
I	C	H	O	R	I	Z	O	N	I
S	O	C	E	R	T	A	I	N	R
I	N	E	T	S	T	A	Y	C	A
B	V	T	X	H	U	P	E	A	G
L	I	Q	U	P	R	N	L	L	E
E	N	U	G	H	E	L	S	M	N
D	C	I	P	L	E	R	M	E	O
O	E	E	X	I	T	O	T	O	T
G	D	T	H	C	L	I	F	F	S

A Introduction

1 These words and phrases are from the article below. Try to match them with their meanings.

a	*ban (on)*	1	a place where rubbish (waste) is buried
b	*breeding grounds*	2	something which is burnt for heat or energy
c	*convert*	3	against the law, unlawful
d	*dispose of*	4	to make use of again
e	*estimate*	5	the top covering or layer of something
f	*fuel*	6	an official rule prohibiting something
g	*landfill site*	7	places where animals, fish etc produce their young
h	*illegal*	8	to throw away, to get rid of
i	*recycle*	9	to guess, to calculate approximately
j	*surface*	10	to change something into something else

2 Check in a dictionary the meaning of any of these words or phrases you do not understand.

B Reading

1 Read this article and fill each gap with the correct form of a word or phrase from **A1**

No more dumping

One of Britain's most serious environmental problems is what to do with millions of used car tyres. 'By their very nature, tyres are difficult to dispose of,' says David Santillo, an environmentalist from Exeter University. 'They are designed not to fall apart while you're driving along the motorway.' The problem will become more serious in the near future when European countries will no longer be allowed to bury tyres in **(a)**_____ .

The problem

- After the **(b)**_____ on the use of landfill sites, new ways will have to be found to dispose of 13 million tyres in Britain every year. By 2021 the number of tyres in use will increase by about 60%.

- Every day, up to 100,000 tyres are taken off cars, vans, trucks, buses and bicycles.

- It is **(c)**_____ that there are now more than 200 million tyres lying around the country.

What to do with old tyres

- The best use of old tyres is to make them into new tyres, but this is expensive, and only 18% are **(d)**_____ in this way.

- 48,500 tonnes are **(e)**_____ into 'crumb rubber', used to make **(f)**_____ for running tracks and children's playgrounds.

- Currently 18% are burnt at high temperatures as **(g)**_____ in the manufacture of cement.

This is becoming the most popular way of disposing of tyres, but it is of increasing concern to environmentalists and scientists.

- Britain sends 26% of its tyres to landfill sites, much less than some other EU countries. France sends almost half, and Spain 58%, but Holland sends none. Britain is now wondering how to **(h)**_____ the extra 13 million tyres once landfill becomes **(i)**_____ .

A new way forward

One new way of re-using old tyres that is being tested around the world is 'tyre reefs'. These are made of old tyres which are tied together and dropped in the sea. It is hoped that they will become successful **(j)**_____ for fish.

2 What do you remember about the article? Answer these questions, then read the article again to check your answers.

a Which countries will not be allowed to use landfill sites to bury tyres?

b How many tyres a day are taken off cars and other vehicles in Britain?

c What percentage of old tyres are made into new tyres?

d Which country mentioned in the article buries the most tyres in landfill sites?

e Where are 'tyre reefs' put?

C Related words

1 Fill the gaps in this chart with words related to the words given. Sometimes there are two words in one group. (X = no useful word at this level.)

Noun	Verb	Adjective	Adverb
a concern	_____	_____	X
b environmentalist	X	environmental	_____
c _____	estimate	X	X
d _____	X	expensive	_____
e _____	X	popular	_____
f _____ scientist	X	_____	_____
g _____	_____	successful	_____

2 Fill the gaps in these sentences with the appropriate form of words you have added to the chart.

a If at first you don't _____, try again.

b As oil prices have risen, small cars have grown in _____.

c According to scientists, landfill sites damage the natural _____.

d What _____ environmentalists is the increase in pollution.

e You don't have to tell me the exact time you will arrive. A rough _____ will be OK.

f _____ does not have the answers to all our problems.

g Elaine must earn a lot. She's always very _____ dressed.

D Phrasal verbs with *fall*

1 Choose the best meaning for *fall apart* in this sentence from the article:
*They are designed not to **fall apart** while you're driving along the motorway.*

a drop off the car

b go down, lose air

c break into pieces

2 Match each of these *fall* verbs with one of the meanings **a–e**.

fall behind   fall down   fall for   fall out   fall through

   a fall in love with
   b move more slowly, make slower progress than other people
   c go wrong (e.g. an arrangement)
   d collapse, no longer be standing (e.g. like a tree or a house)
   e stop being friendly with someone

3 Complete these sentences with the correct form of one of the verbs from **D2**.
   a Unfortunately our plan to have a holiday together has _____ _____.
   b Being off school for three weeks meant that I _____ _____ with my work.
   c I've always loved you. I _____ _____ you the first time we met.
   d After the heavy storms, the bridge was so weak that it _____ _____.
   e My brother and I frequently used to _____ _____ with each other, but we were always friends again by the next day.

E Verbs + prepositions

The article says *... new ways will have to be found to dispose **of** 13 million tyres in Britain every year.*
Fill the gaps in the sentences with one of the prepositions from the box.

> *about / between / from / in / into / of / on / to / with*

   a These days most people *believe* _____ recycling waste material if possible.
   b The government does not *approve* _____ the use of landfill sites for burying old tyres, and I must say I *agree* _____ them.
   c Large old houses in city centres are often *converted* _____ apartments.
   d I *object* _____ breathing other people's cigarette smoke.
   e Customers should *insist* _____ high standards of service from supermarkets.
   f This car *belongs* _____ my father, but I sometimes *borrow* it _____ him.
   g If I had to *choose* _____ walking and driving, I'd walk – it's good exercise.
   h Most people *know* very little _____ environmental problems.

F Prefixes

1 Prefixes often give clues to the meaning of words. For example the prefix **re-** means 'again' or 'back' , so to **re**cycle means 'to use again'. Does **re-** add the meaning 'again' or 'back' to the verbs in these sentences?

   a After three weeks I *returned* the books to the library.
   b I *reread* the question several times but I still did not understand it.
   c After I'd listened to the cassette, I *rewound* it and listened again.
   d The teacher was not satisfied with my work, so I had to *redo* it.
   e They're having to *rebuild* the houses that were damaged in the flood.

2 Match these verb prefixes with the meanings they add.

a	*anti*	1	single, one
b	*bi*	2	half
c	*mis*	3	not enough
d	*mono*	4	later than, after
e	*over*	5	against
f	*post*	6	twice, two
g	*semi-*	7	wrongly, badly
h	*under*	8	too much, more than necessary

3 Complete each sentence with a prefix from **F2**.

a Because of the bad weather, they've _____*poned* the match until next week.

b The teacher sent the boy to the head because he had _____*behaved* in class.

c A _____*detached* house is one which is joined to another house on one side.

d If someone is _____*lingual*, they can speak two languages fluently.

e The food in that restaurant is very good, but they often _____*charge* you.

f I'd hate to do a _____*tonous* job where I had to do the same thing every day.

g People sometimes think she's _____*social*, but actually she's just very shy.

h These potatoes are _____*cooked*. They need to be boiled for at least five more minutes.

EXTENSION

Answer the questions with appropriate nouns from the box below.

a What do you call a word like *you*, *book* or *leave* (but not *fuel*, or *bury*)?
b What do you call someone who is illegally married to two people at the same time?
c What does PS at the end of a letter stand for?
d What is another word for bad luck?
e What should you take if you have been bitten by a poisonous snake?

> antidote / bigamist / misfortune / monosyllable / postscript

G Practice

Read this short article about the use of tyres as fuel. Fill the gaps with the correct form of words from the box. There are two words you do not need to use.

> convert / dispose of / environment / fuel / oil / recycle / smoke / surface / temperature / tyre

Blue Circle, Britain's largest cement maker, uses old **(a)** _____ as a replacement **(b)** _____. The company says that this is a 'win-win' situation for the environment: less **(c)** _____ and coal are used and the tyres are **(d)** _____ instead of being **(e)** _____ in landfill sites. Blue Circle also gains because the 4 million tyres it burns every year save the company about £6 million.

Their own experiments have shown that burning tyres reduces the damage to the local **(f)** _____ by 27%. Tyres which are burned at a very high **(g)** _____ do not produce black **(h)** _____ or an unpleasant smell.

A Introduction

1 These words and phrases are from the article below. Try to match them with their meanings.

a	active	1	probable
b	climate	2	to stop something continuing in the normal way
c	disrupt	3	in danger
d	erupt	4	to say what will happen in the future
e	flow	5	weather conditions
f	fragment	6	not dead, likely to erupt
g	likely	7	to watch and check regularly
h	liquid	8	a small piece
i	monitor	9	to burst or explode
j	predict	10	to move smoothly in one direction
k	at risk	11	like water, oil, milk, etc, not solid

2 Check in a dictionary the meaning of any of these words you do not understand.

B Reading

1 Read the article and fill each gap with the correct form of a word or phrase from **A1**

Predicting eruptions

Today there are many (**a**)_____ volcanoes worldwide and, as the world's population grows, more and more people are living in dangerous volcanic areas. South of Mexico City, Popocatépetl has begun to come to life again, putting a million people (**b**) _____. Another million people living near Naples are threatened by Mount Vesuvius.

What are volcanoes?

Deep inside the Earth, between the (**c**) _____ core and the thin crust at the surface, there is solid rock called the mantle. When rock from the mantle melts, moves to the surface, and releases gases, volcanoes erupt. When we think of a volcanic eruption, we usually imagine red-hot lava (**d**) _____ down a volcano. But falling ash is another problem. In an explosive eruption the liquid rock, 'magma', which has risen to the surface, bursts from the volcano

in a column of ash and fiery (**e**) _____. In a large-scale eruption, the cooled ash and fragments that fall back to Earth can cover vast areas with a thick layer. Severe eruptions can even affect the (**f**) _____, as happened in the case of Mount St Helens in the USA which erupted in 1980 and (**g**) _____ normal weather conditions for months.

Warning signs

Trying to (**h**) _____ when a volcano will (**i**) _____, scientists study what is left behind from past eruptions. They are also skilled at recognising the warning signs. Before an eruption, magma moves nearer the surface and releases gases, which can be measured for changes in quantity and make-up. Volcanologists are becoming very skilled at predicting how (**j**) _____ an eruption is, but it is still very difficult for them to say exactly when it will happen. Monitoring possible eruptions is expensive and, with many volcanoes erupting only every few hundred or thousand years, it is not practical to (**k**) _____ every site.

2 Read the article again and find **one** word to complete each label on this diagram.

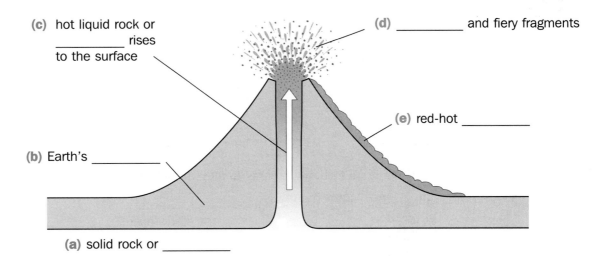

(c) hot liquid rock or _____ rises to the surface

(d) _____ and fiery fragments

(e) red-hot _____

(b) Earth's _____

(a) solid rock or _____

C Related words

1 Fill the gaps in this chart with words related to the words given. Sometimes there are two words in one group. (X = no useful word at this level.)

Noun	Verb	Adjective	Adverb
a _____ _____	_____	active	_____
b _____	disrupt	_____	X
c _____	erupt	X	X
d _____	_____	explosive	_____
e _____	predict	_____	_____
f _____	X	severe	_____
g _____	threaten	_____	_____
h _____	X	_____	violently
i volcano	X	_____	X

2 Fill the gaps in these sentences with the correct forms of words you have added to the chart.

a The bad weather caused severe _____ to the train services.

b Police and politicians are worried about the recent rise in crimes of _____.

c Soon after the car caught fire, the petrol tank _____.

d When business is bad, employees face the _____ of losing their jobs.

e Volcanoes are not _____. We don't know when they are going to erupt.

f The _____ of the storm surprised even the weather experts.

D Adjectives and their opposites

1 Match these adjectives from the article with words that have the opposite meaning.

a	*active (volcano)*	1	small
b	*normal*	2	solid
c	*dangerous*	3	dormant
d	*likely*	4	unusual
e	*liquid*	5	mild
f	*severe*	6	inexperienced
g	*skilled*	7	safe
h	*vast*	8	improbable

2 Add one of the following prefixes to form the opposite of each adjective.

im-   in-   non-   un-

a *active* _____   e *predictable* _____

b *usual* _____   g *expensive* _____

c *likely* _____   f *possible* _____

d *violent* _____   h *practical* _____

3 Use some of the words you have just formed to complete these sentences.

a Theft and shoplifting are examples of _____ crimes.

b At the moment the weather is completely _____ – today it's sunny and yesterday it rained.

c I'm afraid that's a(n) _____ suggestion. We haven't got enough money.

d It's _____ that he'll come now. He's already two hours late.

e They're night birds. It's quite _____ to see them during the day.

f Compared to driving a car, cycling is a(n) _____ way to travel.

E Collocations: 'Size' adjectives + nouns

1 Which nouns in the box can follow these 'size' adjectives?

deep   small   thick   thin   vast

> area / book / business / change / country / feeling / hair / hole / layer / line /
> majority / number / pullover / shirt / water

2 Which collocations from **E1** mean approximately the same as the following?

a strongly-felt emotion   d coins

b something to wear in warm weather   e something to wear in cold weather

c a very large proportion   f a company which employs only a few workers

EXTENSION: Idioms with 'size' adjectives

Match the idioms in these sentences with meanings **1–5**

a If you're late for work again, you'll be *in deep water*.

b We were up until *the small hours* – that's why we're so tired.

c Nothing you say will worry him. He's very *thick-skinned*.

d She wasn't here a minute ago. She just appeared *out of thin air*.

e I'm very grateful to my parents. They've helped me *through thick and thin*.

1 very early in the morning or very late at night
2 in good times and bad times
3 from nowhere
4 in serious trouble
5 not worried by criticism

F Plurals of nouns ending in -o

1 Read these rules. Can you think of any more examples for each group?

a The plural of some common nouns ending in a consonant + -o is **-oes**:

volcano → volcanoes, tomato → tomatoes

b Some exceptions to this rule are abbreviations, foreign words and words ending in a vowel + -o:

photo → photos, peso → pesos, radio → radios

2 For each of these definitions write down the correct word ending in **-oes** or **-os**.

a Famous men everyone admires
b Places where artists and photographers work
c Abbreviation for kilograms
d Cassettes which we can watch films or TV programmes on
e Places where people go to dance to modern music, usually at night

G Practice

Read this short article about planning for the future and fill the gaps with words from the box. There are **two** words you do not need to use.

dangers / eruption / impossible / lava / measure / practical / predict / prevent / safer / severe / volcanic / volcano

Planning for the future

Obviously, it is **(a)**_____ to stop a volcanic **(b)**_____, but there are certain **(c)**_____ steps we can take to reduce the effects. For example, we can make buildings stronger and build protective walls to stop or redirect **(d)**_____ flows. Such efforts can be successful, although they may not help much in the case of a large-scale eruption.

By contrast, protecting future buildings from **(e)**_____ hazards is a simpler task. Before building, we should **(f)**_____ the risk, and if it seems too great, we should try to find a **(g)**_____ place to build.

When a **(h)**_____ comes to life, a few weeks may not be enough time to **(i)**_____ a tragedy. Planning is the key to saving lives. Well before the warning signs occur, people must be educated about the **(j)**_____ of volcanic eruptions.

New carrots

A Introduction

1 These words and phrases are from the article below. Try to match them with their meanings.

a	artificial	1	to affect the way someone thinks or behaves
b	bunch	2	available to buy in the shops
c	commercial	3	to cover a bigger area than before
d	influence	4	normal, not artificial
e	on sale	5	economic, connected with business and finance
f	original	6	a small round thing from which new plants grow
g	seed	7	not real, not natural
h	spread	8	eyesight, the ability to see
i	natural	9	first, what something was like in the beginning
j	vision	10	a collection or group of similar things, e.g. flowers, vegetables

2 Check in a dictionary the meaning of any of these words or phrases you do not understand.

B Reading

1 Read this article and fill each gap with the correct form of a word or phrase from A1.

The future is purple

Five years after a frozen food company tried to encourage children to eat vegetables by covering their carrots in chocolate, supermarkets are now reintroducing carrots in one of their (**a**) _____ colours: purple.

Purple carrots – dark on the outside, orange on the inside – are already (**b**) _____ in shops, while green, yellow, red, white and black varieties may follow. Growers say this change of colour is entirely (**c**) _____, as carrots occurred in many different colours before the Dutch produced an orange variety in the 16th century that became a massive (**d**) _____ success. Temple drawings show that over 4000 years ago the Egyptians had purple-coloured plants thought to be carrots, and researchers have discovered that by the 1300s, purple and yellow varieties of carrot had (**e**) _____ from Afghanistan to Europe and China. Red and white carrots were also grown.

Orange carrots contain high levels of betacarotene, which is a form of vitamin A that improves (**f**) _____ in dim light. Purple carrots also contain anthocyanin, which may help prevent heart disease. The supermarket giant Sainsbury's, which is selling the carrots called Purple Haze, say they are thinking about introducing a rainbow-coloured (**g**) _____ soon.

According to a report in 1999, less than 20% of the vegetable (**h**) _____ available in the early 20th century were commercially grown 100 years later. Over 90% of carrot varieties have been lost. In 1903 there were 287 varieties of carrots being grown, but 80 years later there were only 21 types of carrot seed in the US national seed storage laboratory.

Sainsbury's are hoping for a small change in people's eating habits. A spokesman said: "Hopefully this unusual colour will (**i**) _____ children to eat more vegetables, while parents can be sure that there is nothing (**j**) _____ about the carrots."

2 Decide whether these statements about the information in the article are true (T) or
false (F). Then read the article again to check your answers.

a Carrots have always been orange.   T / F
b Purple carrots are purple in the middle and on the outside.   T / F
c Betacarotene helps to prevent heart disease.   T / F
d Purple and yellow carrots came from Afghanistan.   T / F
e You can buy more types of carrots now than you could 100 years ago. T / F

C Related words

1 Fill the gaps in this chart with words related to the words given. (X = no useful word
at this level.)

Noun	Verb	Adjective	Adverb
a _____	encourage	_____	X
b X	X	_____	entirely
c _____	influence	_____	X
d _____ _____	_____	original	_____
e _____	prevent	_____ _____	X
f storage	_____	X	X
g variety	X	_____ _____	X

2 Fill each gap in these sentences with the correct form of a word you have added
to the chart.

a When the company closes, the _____ workforce will be made redundant,
even the top managers.
b A healthy diet plays an important part in the _____ of disease.
c Employees work best when they get _____ from their boss and their colleagues.
d There are _____ reasons why people prefer orange carrots.
e One of the main _____ in my childhood was my older sister. She was more
important to me than my parents.
f I live in France now, but I come from Scotland _____.
g It isn't necessary to _____ carrots in the fridge.

D Vegetables and colours

1 Check the meaning of any of these vegetables you do not understand.

aubergine / bean / broccoli / cabbage / carrot / cauliflower / courgette /
garlic / onion / pea / potato / mushroom

2 What colours are the vegetables in **D1**? Use words from this box.

> black / blue / brown / green / grey / orange / purple / red / yellow / white

Example: *Carrots are usually orange.*

E Adjective-noun collocations

1 Match these three adjectives with one or more of meanings **a–g** below:

dark   dim   dull

a boring
b not pale or light in colour
c not clear (e.g. something you see or remember)
d not bright (e.g. a light)
e not sharp (e.g. a headache)
f unintelligent, not clever
g with no light (e.g. a room)

2 Which nouns in the box can follow these adjectives?

dark   dim   dull

> colour / eyes / glasses / hair / light / memory / pain / story / student / weather

3 Fill each gap in these sentences with the correct form of a collocation from **E2**.

a I can remember my first day at school quite clearly, but I have very _____ _____ of my life before that.

b The dentist took one of my teeth out yesterday. It's almost better, but I can still feel a _____ _____.

c At first she thought everyone was asleep but then she saw a _____ _____ coming from one of the bedrooms.

d I hope the sun shines when we're on holiday. The _____ has been _____ and wet for the last three weeks.

e Most Japanese and Chinese people have _____ _____ and _____.

f He thought no one would recognise him because he was wearing _____ _____.

4 Replace the words *dark*, *dim* and *dull* in phrases **a–g** with one of these words with the opposite meaning. Some words have more than one possible opposite.

> bright / clear / fair / interesting / light / sharp

a a dull afternoon _____
b dim headlights _____
c a dull pain _____
d dark hair _____
e a dull newspaper _____
f dark green _____
g a dim memory _____

F Numbers and words

These numbers are from the article. Write them in words.

a 4000 _____

b the 1300s _____

c 1999 _____

d 20% _____

e the 20th century _____

f 1903 _____

g 287 _____

EXTENSION: Words and numbers

Read the words and write the numbers.

a twenty-seven point five per cent
b seventeen sixty-two (year)
c fourteen thousand nine hundred and eleven
d three-quarters
e eight-two-oh-double-four-five (phone number)
f six forty-five (time)
g the thirteenth of June (date)
h one point seven five

G Puzzle

Read the clues and complete the puzzle. All the answers are words from this unit.

a A large, round, green and white vegetable
b Intelligent; opposite of *dim* light
c A period of a hundred years
d A noun related to the adverb *originally*
e The noun related to *influential*
f Not clear – like something you cannot remember well
g A group or collection, e.g. flowers, grapes, carrots
h An adjective related to *variety*
i Small round green vegetables
j The opposite of *bright* and *interesting*
k Not real, not natural

18 The writer

A Introduction

1 These words and phrases are from the story below. Try to match them with their meanings.

a	*background*	1	energetic, enthusiastic, showing interest
b	*click*	2	to give something in return for something else
c	*distant*	3	uncivilised, simple
d	*entertain*	4	far away
e	*exchange*	5	information about people, places and situations which helps readers to understand a story
f	*inhabitant*	6	a short stop or break
g	*lively*	7	to become
h	*pause*	8	a small noise, like a light being switched on or off
i	*primitive*	9	someone who lives in a particular place
j	*turn into*	10	to amuse or interest

2 Use your dictionary to check the meaning of any of these words or phrases you do not understand.

B Reading

1 Read this story and fill each gap with the correct form of a word or phrase from **A1**.

Science fiction?

Every month the writers all met to (a) _____ stories and to discuss life as a writer. Their conversations usually (b) _____ storytelling sessions where every writer tried to (c) _____ the others.

Tonight was one of these nights. Laughter and (d) _____ talk filled the warm room. It was getting late, and most of the writers had already told their story. After a brief (e) _____ in the conversation and to everyone's surprise, John started talking. John was a science fiction writer who usually just listened and watched the others, but never participated. This evening, he began his story. Everyone listened.

"I used to live in a house in the country with my family," he began. "One day I started thinking about a new novel, and decided to write the (f) _____ to the story."

"I described a world in a (g) _____ galaxy, with details of the dangerous plants and animals, and suddenly I felt or heard something like a (h) _____, a feeling as if what I wrote had

become real. It was a very strange, but very real feeling. Then I filled this world with half-intelligent, savage creatures who were always fighting terrible wars. I also put strange diseases in many parts of my new world. Again I experienced the 'click', and I was sure that somewhere, very far away, what I wrote had become real."

The listeners leaned closer. "What happened then?", a woman asked. John went on: "I decided to write about myself as one of the (i) _____ of this peculiar world. I described every detail of the life of the new 'me'. I suddenly felt a 'click' which was much stronger than before, and I found myself in my new world."

He paused, and sipped his drink. "In this world I was also a writer. I wrote about my own life and the half-intelligent, (j) _____ people in the world seemed to find what I wrote interesting. They even paid me for it. In this way I managed to earn my living."

The woman smiled and asked: "Well, how did you get back?"

"I didn't get back," he replied. "I'm still here."

2 What do you remember about the story? Make true sentences by matching each beginning with the correct ending.

Beginnings	Endings
a Every month the writers met...	1 science fiction writer.
b John was a ...	2 primitive.
c John didn't usually ...	3 very interested in John's story.
d The people in John's story were ...	4 for writing stories.
e The other writers were ...	5 to tell each other stories.
f In his story, John was paid ...	6 say anything to the other writers.

C Related words

1 Fill the gaps in this chart with words related to the words given. Sometimes there are two words in one group. (X = no useful word at this level.)

Noun	Verb	Adjective	Adverb
a creature _____ *	_____	_____	_____
b _____	describe	_____	X
c _____	X	distant	_____
d _____ _____ *	entertain	_____	_____
e inhabitant*	_____	_____ _____ (opposite)	X
f _____	X	intelligent _____ (opposite)	_____
g laughter	_____	X	X

*These words refer to people.

2 Fill the gaps in these sentences with the appropriate form of words you have added to the chart.

a Films, music and sport are three forms of _____.

b When he finished his story, nobody _____. They didn't think it was funny.

c As far as anyone knows, there is no life on Mars. It is a(n) _____ planet.

d Science fiction writers _____ new worlds from their imagination.

e On a clear day you can see the mountains in the _____. They are actually over 100 kilometres away.

f The police gave a full _____ of the missing person.

D Verb-noun collocations

1 Which nouns in the box can follow these verbs?

earn   gain   win

> experience / your living / the lottery / money / a prize / a race / wages / weight

2 Complete these sentences using verb-noun collocations from **D1**.

a My friend has _____ _____! She got all six numbers right.

b I ate lots of nice food on holiday. That's why I've _____ so much _____ recently.

c I play the saxophone in my spare time, but I _____ my _____ as an accountant.

d When he was at school he _____ several _____ for doing well at sports.

e Nurses work long hours and don't _____ very high _____.

f While she was a teacher she _____ valuable _____ in working with young children.

EXTENSION: Countable and uncountable nouns

1 The nouns *experience* and *weight* can be countable or uncountable.
In each of these sentences, decide whether *experience* or *weight* is countable (C) or uncountable (U).

a *I'm trying to lose weight.*
b *Be careful when you're lifting heavy weights.*
c *That job interview was a most unpleasant experience.*
d *You need experience for this job.*

2 Match the countable and uncountable forms of these words with their meanings.

a a lamb (C)   1 substance used for making furniture
b lamb (U)   2 stuff for writing on
c a glass (C)   3 large group of trees
d glass (U)   4 something you read to find out the news
e a wood (C)   5 substance used for making windows
f wood (U)   6 meat from a young sheep
g a paper (C)   7 something to drink from
h paper (U)   8 young sheep

E Onomatopoeic words

Onomatopoeic words are words that sound like the noise they are describing.
Example: *a click* is a small noise, like a light being switched on or off.

Complete the sentences with appropriate onomatopoeic words from the box.

> crash / creak / growl / jingle / splash / whisper

Note: All these words can be verbs or nouns.

a The children jumped into the swimming pool together, making a great _____.

b The dog _____ and then barked, but it didn't attack me.

c They were _____, so I couldn't hear what they were saying.

d There was a loud _____ as the two cars went into each other.

e The heavy wooden door _____ as she pushed it slowly open.

f As he ran past, you could hear the coins _____ in his pocket.

F Phrasal verbs with *go*

This sentence is in the story: *He **went on**: 'I decided to write about myself...'*
Here *went on* means *continued talking after an interruption.* These are some more phrasal verbs with *go* and their meanings:

go by	pass
go down with	catch (an illness)
go off	become bad or rotten (food or drink)
go through	experience something unpleasant
go without	manage without something you need or want

Now fill the gaps in these sentences with one of the *go* verbs above.

a I know this exam is very important, but you should stop work now and go to bed. It's bad for you to _____ sleep.

b If you leave food out of the fridge in hot weather, it soon _____.

c As a family they've _____ a terrible time. Paul lost his job and they've had to sell their car.

d I feel terrible. I hope I'm not _____ something.

e As the train _____, I thought I saw one of my friends at the window.

G Puzzle

Find the following words in the puzzle. They can be horizontal, vertical or diagonal.

a Water can make this noise.
b A large group of trees
c A short break, stop or hesitation
d To get heavier = to _____ weight.
e Enthusiastic and energetic
f The verb related to *creative* and *creature*
g A person who lives in a place
h The sound of a light switch

```
O  L  C  R  E  A  T  E  F  I
C  L  I  M  A  T  W  O  O  N
C  H  I  V  E  R  O  O  M  H
W  H  A  V  E  T  O  A  R  A
P  L  I  T  I  L  D  O  R  B
A  R  M  S  C  I  Y  P  M  I
U  N  D  E  R  L  N  N  O  T
S  E  G  A  I  N  I  G  N  A
E  X  P  E  R  I  E  C  E  N
R  E  S  P  L  A  S  H  K  T
```

A Introduction

1 These words and phrases are from the story below. Try to match them with their meanings.

a	*by mistake*	**1**	the part of a jacket, shirt etc that covers your arm
b	*denim*	**2**	easy to see, clear, noticeable
c	*charity shop*	**3**	without meaning to, accidentally
d	*crowded*	**4**	an enclosed area of shops where no cars are allowed
e	*panic*	**5**	a shop owned by a charity, which sells things, especially clothes, which people have given
f	*scruffy*	**6**	to have a sudden strong feeling of fear
g	*obvious*	**7**	dirty and untidy
h	*scared*	**8**	thick cloth that jeans are usually made of
i	*shopping mall*	**9**	frightened
j	*sleeve*	**10**	busy, full of people

2 Use your dictionary to check the meaning of any of these words or phrases you do not understand.

B Reading

1 Read the story and fill each gap with the correct form of a word or phrase from **A1**.

The **Big** Blue Shirt

The boy sat there in the **(a)**_____ café, sipping his drink, making it last. His face was sad and thin. Bits of his long brown curly hair were sticking out from under his **(b)**_____ old baseball cap. But it was his big blue **(c)**_____ shirt that really caught my attention.

I was afraid to take my eyes off him in case he disappeared outside into the busy **(d)**_____. I'd never find him again if he did. I had to be sure. Sitting opposite him, I tried not to stare, so that my watching him would not be **(e)**_____. Had he been warned not to speak to strangers? Would he **(f)**_____ if I asked the question I needed to ask?

Suddenly he looked up and I caught his eye. This was my chance. "Excuse me, son. That shirt you're wearing ... did you get it at the **(g)**_____ round the corner?" He suddenly looked **(h)**_____, as if I was a policeman who might arrest him for not being at school. But before he could jump up and run away, I went on: "It was mine, you see. It was my favourite. You can see my name Steve on the **(i)**_____. My wife gave it to the charity shop **(j)**_____. I'd really like to buy it back."

2 What do you remember? Answer these questions, without looking back at the story. Then read the story again to check your answers.

a What colour was the boy's hair?
b What was he wearing on his head?
c Where was the café?
d What did the man ask the boy?
e What was the man's name?
f Where was his name written on the shirt?
g What did the man want to do about the shirt?

C Clothes and parts of clothes

1 Match the correct words from the box with pictures **A–F**.

baseball cap / jacket / shirt / socks / trainers / trousers

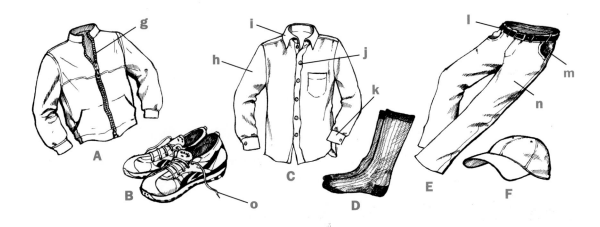

2 Now use these words to label **g–o** above.

belt / button / collar / cuff / lace / leg / pocket / sleeve / zip

D Idioms with *eye*

1 There are two idioms in the story which include the word **eye**. Find them and match them with the correct meanings **a–c**. One meaning does not fit either of the idioms.

a stop looking at someone for a short time
b watch someone for a long time
c make someone notice you

2 Here are some more idioms with the word **eye**. Match them with meanings **1–5** below.

a *keep your eye on* someone / something
b *see eye to eye* (with someone)
c *turn a blind eye to* something
d *be up to your eyes in* something
e *pull the wool over someone's eyes*

1 ignore something / pretend not to notice something
2 be very busy, usually with work of some kind
3 watch or take care of someone / something
4 deceive trick someone
5 have the same opinion as someone

3 Complete these sentences with the appropriate form of one of the **eye** idioms.

  a He and his brother have completely different ideas about things. They never
_____ with each other.

  b Sorry, but I can't come to your party – I'm _____ in work this week.

  c My boss knows we email our friends at work, but he _____ to it.

  d You can't _____. She knows what you're saying is not true.

  e Would you mind _____ the children for half an hour while I go out?

EXTENSION: More things you can wear

Label the picture with words from the box.

> bracelet / earring / glasses / lipstick / nail varnish / necklace / ring / watch

E Adjective order

1 These three phrases are from the story, but only one of them has the words in the correct order. Which one? Rewrite the other phrases in the correct order then check in the story.

  a *long brown curly hair*
  b *old baseball scruffy cap*
  c *denim blue big shirt*

2 Some of the phrases in italics in these sentences are in the wrong order. Rewrite them in the correct order.

   a I love your *bright red silk blouse.*
   b She was wearing *pear-shaped silver beautiful earrings.*
   c He's got *dark short straight hair.*
   d I've bought some *wonderful French new trainers.*
   e They found a *black leather small bag.*

F Meanings of *look*

1 The verb *look* has many meanings. Match the expressions with *look* in these sentences with meanings **1–6** below.

   a The boy *looked up.*
   b She *looked like* my sister.
   c Don't worry. Try to *look on the bright side.*
   d He suddenly *looked* scared.
   e *Look out*!
   f If you're not sure, *look it up* on the Internet.

   1 be careful
   2 appear, seem
   3 try to find information about
   4 be optimistic
   5 resemble
   6 raise your eyes

2 Rewrite these sentences, replacing the words in italics with the appropriate form of one of the expressions from **F1**.

   a There's a car coming! *Be careful!*
   b People say I *resemble* my father.
   c I didn't know what the word 'scared' meant, so I *tried to find the information* in a dictionary.
   d My mother *appeared* older than when I last saw her.
   e I know it's been a bad year for you, but try to *be optimistic* – you're starting a new job next week.

G Practice

Read this short version of *The Big Blue Shirt* and fill the gaps with words from sections **A–F** above.

In the story, the writer's wife had given his favourite **(a)**_____ (*2 words*) shirt to a **(b)**_____ (*2 words*) by **(c)**_____. While he was in a **(d)**_____ in town, the writer saw a young **(e)**_____ wearing his shirt. He didn't speak to him at first because he thought the boy might **(f)**_____ and run **(g)**_____. When he finally asked him about the shirt, the boy was **(h)**_____ because he thought the man was a policeman who was going to **(i)**_____ him.

A Introduction

1 These words and phrases are from the article below. Try to match them with their meanings.

a *fare*	1 a place where you pay money to travel on a road, a bridge, a tunnel, etc
b *frail*	2 in poor condition, in need of decoration (used to describe buildings and places)
c *impulse*	3 a stick with cloth on the end, which is used for washing floors
d *mop*	4 to notice, to see by chance
e *jot down*	5 a sudden feeling which makes you want to do something
f *random*	6 done or happening by chance, not according to a plan
g *rundown*	7 money you pay for a journey
h *spot*	8 to write quickly
i *tollbooth*	9 weak, fragile (used to describe people)

2 Use your dictionary to check the meaning of any of these words or phrases you do not understand.

B Reading

1 Read this article and fill each gap with the correct form of a word or phrase from **A1**.

Kindness is spreading

It's a cold winter day in San Francisco. A woman in a red Honda drives up to the Bay Bridge **(a)**_____. "I'm paying for myself, and for the six cars behind me," she says with a smile, handing over money for seven tickets. One after another, the next six drivers arrive at the booth, dollars in hand, and are told, "Some lady up ahead already paid your **(b)**_____. Have a nice day."

The woman in the Honda, it turned out, had read a message on a friend's fridge: "Practice **(c)**_____ acts of kindness." The phrase impressed her so much that she copied it down.

Judy Foreman **(d)**_____ the same phrase spray-painted on a wall a hundred miles from her home. "I thought it was so inspiring," she said, "that I now write it at the bottom of all my letters." Her husband Frank liked the phrase so much that he put it up on the wall for his seventh-graders, one of whom was the daughter of a local journalist. The journalist put it in her newspaper. Two days later, she heard from Anne Herbert who had read the phrase in her newspaper and **(e)**_____ it _____.

In Portland, Oregon, a man might plunk a coin into a stranger's parking meter just in time. In Patterson, New Jersey, a dozen people with pails and **(f)**_____ might arrive at a **(g)**_____ house and clean it from top to bottom while the **(h)**_____ elderly owners look on, dazed and smiling! In Chicago, a teenage boy may be shovelling snow off the driveway when he feels the same **(i)**_____. "Nobody's looking," he thinks, and clears the snow off the neighbor's driveway too.

A woman in Boston writes "Merry Christmas!" to the tellers on the back of her checks. A man in St Louis, whose car has just been rear-ended by a young woman, waves her away, saying. "It's only a scratch. Don't worry."

Now the phrase is spreading, on bumper stickers, on walls, at the bottom of letters and business cards. As Anne Herbert says: "Kindness can build on itself as much as violence can."

2 The article you have just read is about the idea behind this phrase: 'Practice random acts of kindness.' What does this phrase mean? Choose one of these meanings.

   a *Don't plan what you do. Just do what you feel like.*
   b *Behave generously towards other people with no plan in mind.*
   c *Try to shock and surprise people by doing unexpected things.*

3 What do you remember about the article? Make true sentences by matching each beginning with the correct ending.

Beginnings	Endings
a The woman in San Francisco …	1 to prevent someone from getting a parking fine.
b One of the children in Frank Foreman's class …	2 didn't want people to see him helping his neighbours.
c The Portland man wanted …	3 when people came and cleaned their house for them.
d The old people in New Jersey were surprised …	4 was driving a red car.
e The teenager in Chicago …	5 was the daughter of a journalist.

C Word groups

1 In the following groups of words, one word is a general word and the others are examples of this general word.

Example: *coffee / **drink** / tea / water*

Which are the general words in these groups?

   a *bus / car / lorry / vehicle*
   b *language / phrase / sentence / word*
   c *bed / chair / furniture / table*
   d *instrument / piano / trumpet / violin*
   e *rose / flower / poppy / tulip*

2 Add two more words to each group in C1.

D American English

1 The article you have read is written in American English. Match these words from the article with the correct meaning and with the British English equivalent if there is one.

American English	Meaning	British English
a *driveway*	1 a water container	*plonk*
b *pail*	2 to put in or down heavily without taking care	*year seven pupil*
c *plunk*	3 to drive into the back of the car in front of you	*drive*
d *rear-end*	4 a child in the seventh year of education	*cashier*
e *seventh-grader*	5 a bank employee who accepts or pays out money	*bucket*
f *teller*	6 a wide path beside your house where you can park your car	no equivalent word

2 How are these two American words from the article spelled in British English?

a *a check*

b *to practice*

E Describing periods of time

The first *random act of kindness* in the article took place on a *cold winter day.*. Three-word phrases like this are often used to describe periods of time. Make up a three-word phrase to describe each of the following.

a It's 2 p.m. The weather is warm and it's summer. It's a _____

b The evening is cool and the season is autumn. It's a _____

c It's spring. The sun is shining brightly and it's 8 a.m. It's a _____

d Our holiday in the summer lasts a long time this year. We're having a

_____

e It's cold. It's 11 p.m. The month is December. It's a _____

F Phrasal verbs with *hand*

1 The article tells us that the woman in the red car **handed over** money for seven tickets. Match each of these *hand* verbs with one of the meanings **a–d**.

hand back   hand in   hand out   hand over

a give something to somebody so that it belongs to them
b give things to everybody in a group
c give a piece of work to a teacher to be marked or corrected
d return something you have borrowed from someone

2 Now fill the gaps in these sentences with the correct form of one of the *hand* verbs from **F1**.

a The students have got to _____ _____ their homework on Thursday morning.

b She looked closely at the photograph the police officer had given her and then

_____ it _____.

c The teacher asked David to _____ _____ the papers.

d The bank robbers told the cashier to _____ _____ the money.

EXTENSION: Idioms with *hand*

1 Match each idiom with the correct meaning **1–4**.

a *Hands off!*
b *have your hands full*
c *out of hand*
d *lend someone a hand*

1 to help someone
2 difficult to control
3 to be very busy, to have a lot of work to do
4 Don't touch!

2 Complete these sentences with the correct form of one of the *hand* idioms.

   a The children soon get _____ if you don't watch them.

   b You look terribly busy. Can I _____ you _____?

   c _____ the food! I'll let you know when it's time for lunch!

   d I'm afraid I can't help you at the moment. I've got _____ looking after the visitors.

G Puzzle

Read the clues and complete the puzzle. All the answers are words from this unit.

a Something we use to carry water in

b A *tulip* is a kind of _____.

c A sudden desire to do something

d The American English word for a cashier in a bank

e To *hand* _____ means to return something you have borrowed.

f Not according to a plan, by chance

g To _____ *down* means to write something quickly.

h To notice or see

i Cars and buses are two different kinds of _____.

j Drivers pay money to use a bridge at a _____.

Review 1 (Units 1–4)

1 Related words
Fill each gap with a word related to the word in capitals. The first one has been done for you.

a Many people find TV soap operas _addictive_. They can't stop watching them. ADDICT

b Even the most well-known celebrities need their _____ from time to time. PRIVATE

c Last year there was a two per cent _____ in the population. GROW

d Millions of _____ come to Britain every year. VISIT

e Holidays are my favourite way of escaping from _____. REAL

f As he started to speak, there was complete _____ in the room. SILENT

g Alex is training to be an _____ . ELECTRIC

h The house was full of _____ antique furniture and paintings. VALUE

2 Verb-noun collocations
Complete the sentences with the correct form of one of these verbs. You will need to use one of the verbs twice.

> hold / keep / lose / save / spend / waste / win

a I know I should have been more careful, but don't _____ your temper!

b Instead of walking, why don't we _____ time and take a taxi?

c When they close the factory, the employees all expect to _____ their jobs.

d Don't _____ time watching TV – you should be revising for your exam.

e Email is one of the cheapest ways of _____ in contact with people in other countries.

f Do you know where tomorrow's meeting is being _____?

g Can you lend me some money? I've _____ all mine.

h The Democratic Party were very lucky to _____ the election.

3 Make and do
Complete the sentences with the correct form of *make* or *do*.

a He finished the whole exam in thirty minutes and _____ no mistakes.

b Stop _____ so much noise – I'm on the phone.

c Is it my turn to _____ the cooking tonight?

d Are you going to be long? I've got three phone calls to _____.

e I'll _____ my best to persuade him not to leave.

f Excuse me, can I _____ a suggestion?

g You can't have it both ways – you've just got to _____ a decision.

4 Adjectives
Choose the correct adjectives in these sentences.

a We're going to buy a new *electric / electrical* cooker.

b I love going to the theatre but I'm afraid I can't afford *expensive / valuable* seats.

c Walking is certainly the most *economic / economical* way of travelling.

d Her coat was made of *cheap / free* imitation leather.

e It was very *irrelevant / irresponsible* of you to drive through a red light.

5 Adjective opposites
Add prefixes to these adjectives to make their opposites.

a attractive
b polite
c mature
d legal
e intentional

6 Odd one out
Which word or phrase is the odd one out in each group? Why? The first one is done as an example.

a apple / banana / carrot / orange (*The others are **fruits**.*)

b keys / ring tone / piano / screen

c folk / jazz / rock / track

d band / cassette / CD / mini-disc

e amazing / angry / surprising / unexpected

f cellphone / highway / number plate / trash

Review 2 (Units 5–8)

1 Verb-noun collocations

Make phrases to match definitions **a–f** below. Use one of these verbs and a noun or phrase from the box.

cut   find   have

breakfast / someone guilty / prices / a shower / taxes / your way

a A jury in a court of law can decide to do this.
b You manage to get to the place you want to go to.
c What a shopkeeper can do if things in his / her shop are too expensive.
d You do this if you are hungry when you get up in the morning.
e A government can do this if it wants to be more popular with people.
f You might do this after a hot, tiring day at work.

2 Adjective-noun collocations

Choose the best adjective in each of these sentences.

a David Bellamy is one of the world's *leading / natural / positive* experts on conservation.

b The police are sure he committed the crime, but they can't arrest him because they have no *natural / concrete / mental* evidence.

c That's a(n) *enthusiastic / brilliant / leading* idea! Let's do it!

d These days many sports are played at night under *natural / physical / artificial* light.

e Old people often have an excellent *short-term / mental / long-term* memory, but can't remember what they did yesterday.

f He's such a(n) *enthusiastic / leading / inspiring* politician that thousands of people come to hear him speak.

3 Phrasal verbs

Complete the sentences with the correct form of a phrasal verb from the box.

carry on / carry out / come up with / put up with / set off / set up

a What time shall we _____ tomorrow? We have to be there by lunchtime.

b Is that really the best idea you can _____?

c Don't blame me. I'm just _____ the instructions my boss gave me.

d I'll have to see the dentist. I can't _____ this toothache any longer.

e The government has _____ a new committee to look into the rise in crime.

f Shall I stop now or shall I _____ until I've finished?

4 Related words

Fill each gap with a word related to the word in capitals.

a The character Indiana Jones is an archaeologist and _____. EXPLORE

b I was quite good at practical subjects at school, but I didn't understand some of the _____ background. THEORY

c The better the working conditions, the higher the workers' _____. PRODUCE

d I can't study if there's any noise – it interferes with my _____. CONCENTRATE

e People recognised Mozart's _____ when he was a young child. BRILLIANT

5 Prepositions

Complete the sentences with prepositions from the box. You will need to use some prepositions twice.

for / from / in / of / on / with

a You can't rely _____ warm weather, so you'd better take a coat.

b The children went out into the garden and filled their pockets _____ apples.

c I hope you succeed _____ getting the job you want.

d After finishing the marathon he collapsed – he was suffering _____ exhaustion.

e Thank you _____ inviting me to your party.

f Her letters always smelt _____ expensive perfume.

g He should have passed the exam. He has no explanation _____ his failure.

h They have no interest _____ music of any kind.

Review 3 (Units 9–12)

1 Related words
Fill each gap with a word related to the word in capitals.

a Environmental groups are trying to prevent the _____ of the rainforests. DESTROY

b Taxi drivers should have detailed _____ of the area they work in. KNOW

c The young Japanese violinist gave a brilliant _____. PERFORM

d John's parents watched _____ as their son received his prize. PRIDE

e There's been a 10% _____ in the price of petrol this year. REDUCE

f The man was kept at the police station overnight for his own _____. SAFE

2 Adjective-noun collocations
Match adjectives from box **A** with nouns from box **B**. Then use the pairs of words to complete the sentences.

> **A** common / hard / heavy / lasting / normal / public / sharp / strong

> **B** behaviour / coffee / effect / increase / luck / opinion / rain / sight

a If I'm feeling sleepy in the morning, I have a cup of _____ _____ to wake me up.

b There's been a _____ _____ in compensation claims.

c Politicians are quite unpopular at the moment. It's because they don't listen to _____ _____.

d Young children with mobile phones are a _____ _____ these days.

e I don't care what you say: standing in the middle of the road and screaming is not _____ _____.

f Seeing that terrible accident had a _____ _____ on Debbie.

g The match had to be postponed because of the _____ _____. It was _____ _____ on people who had already bought tickets.

3 Verb-noun collocations
Fill each gap with a verb from the box.

> catch / drive / make / miss / pay / ride / take / travel

a I ran as fast as I could because I thought I was going to _____ the bus.

b Photographers can _____ a very good living by selling pictures of famous people to the newspapers.

c I just wish you'd _____ the doctor's advice and stop smoking.

d If you leave now, you could _____ the half-past eight train.

e If I'm going somewhere on business, I prefer to _____ by plane.

f I learned to _____ a bike when I was six years old.

g I have to _____ the rent every Friday evening.

4 Choose the correct word
Choose the correct words in these sentences.

a My sister was really *annoyed / annoying* when she found out that I'd been reading her email.

b The weather was terrible, so she was really grateful *for / to* the offer of a lift.

c I've just won £25,000 on the lottery – my friends are *green / red* with envy.

d Don't be afraid *for / of* the dog – he won't hurt you.

e It's nobody's *blame / fault*. It was just an accident.

f This coffee's terribly *weak / week*.

g Don't *blame / fault* me. I wasn't even there.

5 Compound adjectives
Which compound adjectives can be used to describe these people and things? The first one has been done for you.

a Someone who writes with their *right hand*.
  right-handed

b A person who has *short hair*.

c A meal that you *cook* at *home*.

d A person who *looks healthy*.

e A person with *blue eyes*.

f Something which is the same *shape* as a *heart*.

Review 4 (Units 13–16)

1 Phrasal verbs
Choose the correct phrasal verb in each sentence.

a That's a really difficult problem. I'll need more time to *round up / work out* the answer.

b It was difficult to *make off / make out* the road signs because of the fog.

c The excuse he *made for / made up* was impossible to believe.

d I always get on well with my parents. We've never *fallen out / fallen behind*.

e The old cottage *fell down / fell through* after the heavy lorry crashed into it.

2 More phrasal verbs
Complete each sentence with the correct form of a phrasal verb from the box.

> come from / come out with / come round /
> come up / come up against / come up with

a You're not American, are you? Where do you _____?

b Some old friends will be here tomorrow. Why don't you _____ and see them?

c You know that problem we've got? Well, I've _____ the perfect solution.

d Everything was going well until I _____ a difficulty I hadn't expected.

e I can't stay long. Something important has just _____ at work.

3 Related words
Fill each gap with a word related to the word in capitals.

a You could hear the _____ 50 kilometres away. EXPLODE

b The overnight rain has caused flooding and general _____. DISRUPT

c If you receive a _____ letter you should inform the police immediately. THREAT

d The weekend sport has been _____ affected by the bad weather. SEVERE

e In recent years organic food has gained in _____. POPULAR

f United are definitely going to win the cup. That's my _____. PREDICT

g Dumping rubbish can cause serious _____ damage. ENVIRONMENT

h The _____ of the volcano came as a complete surprise. ERUPT

4 Prepositions
Choose the correct prepositions in these sentences.

a Does this book belong *to / with* you?

b My parents don't approve *about / of* me smoking.

c I'd love to live *in / on* the coast.

d I object *about / to* people using their mobile phones while they're driving.

e I'm sorry but I can't agree *to / with* you – I think you're quite wrong.

f Look! There's a helicopter *over / up* the house!

5 True or false?
Decide if each sentence is true (T) or false (F).

a A *cold fish* is someone who has a secret life.

b A *guinea pig* is someone who never stops doing things.

c A young lion is called a *cub*.

d A young horse is called a *lamb*.

e A *resident* is someone who lives in a particular place.

f If someone is *bilingual* it means they are fluent in three languages.

g If something is *overcooked*, it hasn't been cooked enough.

h The plural of *radio* is *radioes*.

i The opposite of an *active* volcano is a *non-active* volcano.

j The opposite of *expensive* is *inexpensive*.

6 Confusing words
Choose the correct words in these sentences.

a I saw Emma arrive but I didn't *notice / stare at* what she was wearing.

b That's a really *deep / thick* book – it would take weeks to read it.

c Is a twenty-pound note okay? I'm afraid I haven't got any *small / thin* change.

d Did you *notice / see* the news on TV yesterday?

e The *thick / vast* majority of the population are hooked on soap operas.

f I know he has a strange hairstyle, but don't *stare / watch* – it's rude.

Review 5 (Units 17-20)

1 Related words

Fill each gap with a word related to the word in capitals.

a He's one of the most _____ people I've ever met. **CREATE**

b We could hear _____ coming from the classroom as the teacher told the class a story. **LAUGH**

c The oldest _____ in the village will be 100 next month. **INHABIT**

d Most children do well at school if they get _____ from their parents and teachers. **ENCOURAGE**

e This year the police are concentrating on crime _____. **PREVENT**

f Can you give me a _____ of the man you saw coming out of the bank? **DESCRIBE**

g Bill Clinton was one of the most _____ politicians of the 1990s. **INFLUENCE**

h The latest CD by the New Symphony Orchestra shows great _____. **ORIGIN**

i I've always enjoyed live _____ far more than films or television. **ENTERTAIN**

2 Phrasal verbs

Make phrasal verbs with **go** and **hand** and words from the box to complete the sentences.

> *back / by / down / in / off / out / over / through / without*

a There was no coffee left, so we had to _____ _____.

b The teacher asked me to _____ _____ the new textbooks to the class.

c I saw the bus _____ _____, but I didn't recognise any of the passengers on it.

d The child admitted he'd taken the chocolate and reluctantly _____ it _____ to his mother.

e I feel okay, but half of my class has _____ _____ with flu.

f I'm sorry you've lost your job, but I know what you're _____ _____ – the same thing happened to me three years ago.

g How old is this milk? I think it's _____ _____.

3 Adjective-noun collocations

Choose the correct adjectives in these sentences.

a Why are you wearing those *dark / dim* glasses? It isn't sunny.

b I've had a *dim / dull* pain in my leg since I fell over last week.

c I can hardly remember my first day at school. It's just a *dark / dim* memory.

d That was a really *dim / dull* film. I nearly fell asleep halfway through.

e My sister has got *dark / dim* brown hair.

4 Adjective order

Put the adjectives in italics in these sentences into the correct order.

a My brother has a(n) *American fantastic silver-grey* car.

b I've just bought a(n) *green glass tall* vase.

c My mother's got *dark curly short* hair.

d She'll probably be wearing a(n) *old woollen brown* pullover.

e He usually wears a(n) *incredible gold large* ring.

5 True or false?

Decide if each sentence is true (T) or false (F).

a To *whisper* means to speak very quietly.

b If you drop something heavy into water, it makes a *crash*.

c Some animals *growl* when they are angry.

d If you *pull the wool over someone's eyes*, it means you pretend not to notice them.

e If you *see eye to eye with someone*, it means you trick or deceive them.

f The British English for *driveway* is *motorway*.

g The American English for *cashier* is *teller*.

h A *lorry* is a kind of *vehicle*.

i You can play a *trumpet*.

j A *collar* is something you find on a shoe.

Adjective collocations

Numbers are unit numbers.

artificial	light **5**
bright	afternoon / headlights / green **17**
brilliant	expert / idea / politician / teacher **6**
cheap	fare / gift / holiday / imitation / newspaper / seat / ticket **2**
clear	afternoon / memory **17**
common	effect / flower / name / sight **10**
concrete	effect / evidence / solution **7**
dark	colour / eyes / glasses / hair **17**
deep	feeling / hole / water **16**
dim	light / memory / student **17**
dull	colour / hair / pain / story / student / weather **17**
enthusiastic	expert / politician / teacher / worker **6**
expensive	fare / gift / holiday / mistake / newspaper / seat / ticket **2**
fair	hair **17**
free	fare / gift / holiday / information / newspaper / seat / ticket **2**
general	election / interest / knowledge / rule **12**
hard	decision / drugs / luck / work **9**
heavy	rain / smoker / traffic / work **9**
inspiring	idea / meeting / politician / teacher **6**
interesting	afternoon / newspaper **17**
lasting	effect / impression / relationship **10**
leading	expert / politician **6**
light	hair / green **17**
long-term	effect / memory **5**
mental	ability **5**
natural	ability / effect / light **5**
negative	effect **5**
normal	behaviour / day / price / relations / way **12**
physical	ability / effect / evidence **5**
positive	effect / evidence **5**
productive	meeting / worker **6**
public	health / holiday / interest / knowledge / opinion / relations **12**
sharp	bend / contrast / increase / knife / teeth **10**
	pain **17**
short-term	effect / memory **5**
small	area / book / business / change / country / hole / majority / number **16**
strong	coffee / leader / opinion / taste / wind **9**
thick	book / hair / layer / line / pullover / shirt **16**
thin	book / hair / layer / line / pullover / shirt **16**
valuable	experience / gift / information **2**
vast	area / country / majority / number **16**

afraid of **12**	**loaded** with **12**
available for **12**	**necessary** for **12**
equivalent to **12**	**open** to **12**
good at / for **12**	**opposed** to **12**
grateful for **12**	**worried** about **12**

Verb collocations

Numbers are unit numbers.

catch	someone's attention / a bus / a coach / a criminal / flu / a plane / what someone says / someone doing something / a train **10**
change	(TV) channels / your clothes / currency / jobs / your mind / the subject / trains **1**
cut	bread / costs / prices / a scene from a film / taxes **8**
do	your best / business with someone / the cooking / a crossword / damage / exercises / housework / a job / a painting / the shopping **4**
drive	a bus / a car / a coach / a taxi / a train **10**
earn	your living / money / wages **18**
exchange	glances / greetings / ideas / information / phone numbers **1**
find	the answer to a question / a cure for a disease / the solution to a problem / your way **8**
gain	experience / weight **18**
go for	a bicycle ride / a drink / a drive / a picnic / a run / a swim **1**
have	a bath / a break / breakfast / dinner / a holiday / a rest / a shower **8**
hold	a conversation / an election / a meeting / an opinion **1**
keep	in contact with / your job / your temper **1**
kill	someone / time **3**
lose	contact with someone / an election / interest in / your job / sight of / your temper / your way **1**
make	a decision / an effort / a mistake / a noise / someone an offer / a phone call / progress / room for / a suggestion / trouble **4**
	fun of / a joke / money / notes / a profit **11**
	a scene **19**
miss	a boat / a bus / a coach / a plane / a train **10**
offer	advice / someone a drink / an explanation / information / someone a lift / an opinion **1**
pay	fees / money / rent / tax(es) **11**
play	a CD / chess / football / the piano / a trick on someone **3**
press	a button / a key / a switch **3**
ride	a bicycle / a horse / a motorbike **10**
save	energy / food / money / someone / time **3**
send	a letter / a message / money / a present / a signal **3**
spend	energy / your life / money / time **3**
take	advice / care / an exam / a joke / medicine / notes / responsibility for **11**
travel by	bicycle / boat / bus / car / coach / motorbike / plane / taxi / train **10**
waste	energy / food / your life / money / time **3**
win	an election **1**
	the lottery / money / a prize / a race / a war **18**

agree with **15**	fill with **7**
approve of **15**	focus on **6**
associate with **5**	insist on **15**
believe in **15**	know about **15**
belong to **15**	object to **15**
blame for **11**	pay for **7**
borrow from **15**	protest against **4**
choose between **15**	rely on **7**
consist of **12**	smell of **7**
convert into **15**	succeed in **7**
depend on **7**	suffer from **7**
dispose of **15**	thank someone for **7**

Index

Numbers are unit numbers.

Key

1 A day without the Internet

A Introduction
1
- a 9
- b 6
- c 1
- d 10
- e 2
- f 4
- g 5
- h 3
- i 8
- j 7

B Reading
- a virtual
- b junk
- c isolates
- d big business
- e researchers
- f mouse
- g event
- h risky
- i controversial
- j passively

C Related words
1
- a reality, really
- b addiction, addict
- c damage, damaging
- d communication, communicative, communicatively
- e contact
- f visit, visit
- g perfection, perfect, perfectly
- h excitement, excite, excited
- i risk, risk, riskily

2
- a addict
- b risk
- c visit
- d communicative
- e damage
- f contact
- g excited

D The suffix -free
alcohol-free: drink / lager / wine
duty-free: cigarettes / drink / goods / lager / petrol / wine
fat-free: yoghurt
lead-free: paint / petrol
rent-free: accommodation / holiday
trouble-free: holiday / journey

EXTENSION 1
1 Addictions
A chocoholic is addicted to eating chocolate.
A shopaholic is addicted to shopping.
A workaholic is addicted to working.

2 *Go for*
We can go for: a bicycle ride / a drink / a picnic / a run / a swim

E Verb-noun collocations
1 **exchange**: glances / greetings / ideas / information / phone numbers
hold: a conversation / an election / a meeting / an opinion
lose: contact with / an election / interest in / your job / sight of / your temper / your way
offer: advice / someone a drink / an explanation / information / someone a lift / an opinion

2
- a 4, offered
- b 8, holding
- c 1, lose
- d 3, lost
- e 7, offer
- f 2, exchange
- g 6, holding
- h 5, offers

EXTENSION 2
1 Opposites of *lose*
- a keep
- b find
- c keep
- d keep
- e win

2 Collocations with *change*
- a trains
- b your clothes
- c currency
- d your mind
- e the subject
- f jobs
- g channels

F Phrasal verbs with *turn*
1
- a turn up
- b turn up
- c turn off
- d turn on
- e turn off
- f turn down
- g turn down

2
- a turn it down
- b turn off
- c turned up
- d turn the heater on / up
- e turned him down

G Practice
- a addicted
- b virtual
- c workaholic
- d put down
- e turn off
- f contact
- g event
- h real
- i going for
- j risky

2 The future of music

A Introduction
1
- a 8
- b 6
- c 7
- d 10
- e 2
- f 9
- g 1
- h 5
- i 4
- j 3

B Reading
1
- a duplicate
- b tunes
- c flexible
- d consumers
- e mass
- f value
- g accessible
- h luxury
- i download
- j select

2
- a F It was invented in the 19th century.
- b F It made it less flexible – it fixed it.
- c F Analog copies were cheap, but digital copies are free.

d T '... the only truly valuable things are those which cannot be copied.'

e F 'Music will continue to be sold, because it will be easier to buy music you really like than to find it for free.'

C Related words

1 a access, access
b electrician
c industry, industrialise, industrialised
d luxurious
e performer, perform
f repetition, repetitive
g selection, selective
h technologist, technological
i transformation
j value

2 a industry
b performed
c luxurious
d electric
e selection
f repetitive

EXTENSION: Adjective pairs

a economical
b historic
c electric
d economic
e electrical
f historical

D Adjective-noun collocations

1 cheap: fares / gift / holiday / imitation / newspaper / seat / ticket
expensive: fare / gift / holiday / mistake / newspaper / seat / ticket
free: fares / gift / holiday / information / newspaper / seat / ticket
valuable: experience / gift / information / (ticket)

2 a free gift
b cheap imitation
c valuable information
d expensive mistake
e free newspapers
f valuable experience
g cheap seats / tickets
h expensive holiday

E Music words

1 Kinds of music: *jazz, opera, pop, rock*
People: *band, composer, orchestra, singer*
Words connected with recordings: *cassette, mini-disc, studio, track*
Other words: *performance, rhythm, song, tune*

3 Other possible words
Kinds of music: *classical, country, reggae, world music*
People: *drummer, guitarist, musician, pianist, player*
Words connected with recordings: *CD cover / case, recording, sound engineer*
Other words: *melody, words / lyrics*

F Word groups

a *Energy* is the general word. *Electricity, gas, nuclear power and solar power* are different kinds of energy.

b *Entertainment* is the general word. *Cinema, theatre and television* are different kinds of entertainment.

c *Meal* is the general word. *Breakfast, dinner, lunch and supper* are different meals.

d *Time* is the general word. *Century, month, week and year* are different lengths of time.

e *Recording* is the general word. *Cassette, CD, DVD and mini-disc* are different kinds of recording.

G Puzzle

a expensive, cheap
b consumer
c select
d folk
e flexible
f technologist, electrician
g tune
h economic
i repetition
j luxurious
k supper
l video

3 Mobile phones

A Introduction

1 a A watch does not have a screen. It has a *face* or a *digital display*.
b A video recorder does not have *keys*. It has *buttons*.

2 a peaktime
b emergencies
c communicating
d rings
e compose
f text
g characters
h companies
i Pre-paid

B Reading

a emergencies
b text
c communicate
d companies
e pre-paid
f peaktime
g characters
h ring
i keys
j compose
k screens

C Verb-noun collocations

1 play: a CD / chess / football / the piano / a trick on someone
press: a button / a key / a switch
send: a CD / a letter / a message / money / a present / a signal
spend: energy / money / time

2 a 4 press
b 8 've spent
c 1 playing

d 7 play
e 2 sent
f 6 press
g 5 played
h 3 spent

EXTENSION 1

The following words should be ticked:
kill: a person
save: energy, food, a person, money
spend: energy, your life, money
waste: energy, food, your life, money

D Compound nouns

1 *mobile phone* adjective + noun
street corner noun + noun
text messaging noun + -ing
school classroom noun + noun + noun
phone companies noun + noun
phone calls noun + noun
under-18s preposition + noun
picture message noun + noun
pop songs noun + noun, or adjective + noun (if *pop* is seen as short for *popular*)

2 a a phone conversation
b the over-30s
c a ring tone
d a public phone box
e an answerphone message

E Related words

1 a mobility / mobile (phone), immobile
b imagination, imaginary / imaginative, unimaginative
c intend, intentional, unintentional
d growth, grow
e attract, attractive, unattractive
f silence, silence
g secret / secrecy
h privacy
i immediacy
2 a intentional
b growth
c attract
d silence
e imaginary
f privacy

EXTENSION 2: Adjectives and their opposites

Some adjectives which begin with *m* add *im-*, e.g.
mobile / mature / moral / modest
Some adjectives which begin with *l* add *il-*, e.g.
legal / legible / logical
Some adjectives which begin with *r* add *ir-*, e.g.
responsible / rational / regular
Some adjectives which begin with *p* add *im-*, e.g.
polite / patient / possible / personal / practical
a irregular
b impatient
c illegible
d immature
e irrelevant

F Practice

a growth
b under
c attractive
d communicate / communicating
e phoning
f sending
g messages
h spending

4 Camera rage in Hawaii

A Introduction

1 a 3 **b** 9 **c** 6 **d** 10
e 7 **f** 1 **g** 8 **h** 4
i 2 **j** 5

B Reading

1 a are protesting against
b unmarked
c speed
d furious
e gestures
f major
g residential
h drops
i packs
j rage
2 a In unmarked vans
b Morning radio shows
c 55 mph
d They cover their license plates; they drive in packs (close to each other, so that the cameras cannot see their plates).
e Nearly 1,300

C Strong adjectives

1 a irritated / angry / furious
b cool / cold / freezing
c satisfactory / good / excellent
d sleepy / tired / exhausted
e unexpected / surprising / amazing
2 a exhausted
b freezing
c amazing
d furious
e excellent

EXTENSION 1: Related words

a amazement
b coolness
c excellence
d fury
e goodness
f irritation
g satisfaction
h surprise

D American English

1 a 5
b 3
c 6
d 1
e 4
f 2
2 b centre
c humor
d licence
e catalog
f travelled

E Verb-noun collocations: *Make* and *do*

1 make: a decision / an effort / a mistake / a noise / someone an offer / a phone call / progress / room for / a suggestion / trouble
do: your best / business with someone / the cooking / a crossword / damage / exercises / housework / a job / a painting / the shopping
2 a do the shopping
b ('ve) made a terrible mistake
c make a much bigger effort

d did / has done a lot of damage
e make room for
f make a suggestion
g made so much noise

EXTENSION 2: Meanings of *make* and *do*
a earn
b travel
c spend
d come to / equal
e come to
f cut or style

F Verb-adverb collocations
1 **drive**: carefully / carelessly / dangerously / fast / quickly / slowly
sleep: heavily / lightly / well
speak: carefully / carelessly / clearly / fast / loudly / noisily / quickly / slowly
walk: briskly / carefully / carelessly / fast / heavily / lightly / loudly / noisily / quickly / slowly
work: carefully / carelessly / fast / hard / loudly / noisily / quickly / slowly
2 a speak more clearly / slowly
b walk / drive a little more quickly
c driving fast / dangerously / carelessly
d sleeps heavily / well
e works hard / fast / quickly / carefully
3 a a careful driver
b a clear speaker
c a light sleeper
d a good worker
e a slow walker

G Puzzle

```
                 k
a      R E S I D E N T I A L
b              R A G E
c            T R A S H
d        F U R I O U S
e        G E S T U R E
f              C A R E F U L L Y
g    E X C E L L E N T
h            A M A Z I N G
i          C A T A L O G
j        C E L L P H O N E
```

5 Is chewing gum good for you?

A Introduction
1 a 3
b 6
c 8
d 2
e 7
f 1
g 4
h 5

B Reading
1 a F
b T
c F
d T
e F
2 a associated
b mental
c imitation
d assessment
e exploring
f theories
g evidence
h concentration

C Related words
1 a assessor, assess
b concentrate, concentrated
c evident, evidently
d exploration, explorer, explorative
e imitator, imitate, imitative
f association
g mentality, mentally
h theoretical, theoretically
2 a explorer
b imitate
c evidently
d concentrate
e Theoretically
f mentally

D Adjective-noun collocations
1 a 5
b 4
c 1
d 3
e 2
2 mental / physical / natural / *ability*
long-term / short-term / natural / physical / positive / negative *effects*
physical / positive / concrete *evidence*
natural / artificial *light*
long-term / short-term *memory*
3 a natural ability
b concrete evidence
c positive effects
d short-term memory
e artificial light

EXTENSION: 'Memory' verbs
1 a 4
b 3
c 5
d 2
e 1
2 a recognise
b memorising
c reminds
d recall
e remind

E Phrasal verbs with *carry*
a carrying out
b carry through
c carry on
d carried it off
e carried away

F Nouns + prepositions
a in
b on
c to
d between
e in
f on
g for
h into, between
i for

G Practice
a memory
b recognise
c remember
d short-term
e remember / recall
f recall / remember
g improvement
h concentrate
i mental

6 Job stress in Sweden

A Introduction
1 a 7
b 8
c 6
d 10
e 2
f 1

g 4
h 9
i 5
j 3

B Reading
a burned out
b casualties
c experience
d experts
e clinic
f high-pressure
g campaigns
h focus on
i sick
j productive

C Adjective-noun collocations
1 brilliant: expert / idea / politician / teacher
enthusiastic: expert / politician / teacher / worker
inspiring: idea / meeting / politician / teacher
leading: expert / politician
2 a leading experts
b brilliant idea
c inspiring teacher
d leading politicians
e enthusiastic workers

D Related words
a brilliance, brilliantly
b enthusiasm / enthusiast, enthuse, enthusiastically
c inspiration, inspire
d leader, lead
e product / productivity / producer, produce, productively

EXTENSION 1: *High- / Low-*
a high-speed car
b low-fat food
c high-risk sports
d low-cost housing
e high-class hotel
f high-level meeting
g low-lying land

E Phrasal verbs with *out*
a run out
b tires me out
c knocked out
d dying out
e blew out
f sold out

EXTENSION 2
a 2
b 4

c 1
d 3

F Three-part phrasal verbs
a 5
b 3
c 2
d 1
e 4
f 6

G Confusing words
a *effect* This is a noun. *Affect* is a verb = *to have an effect on.*
b *experiments* This means tests. *Experiences* = things that happen to people.
c *home* Home is the place you live. *A house* is a particular kind of building.
d *sensitive* This means delicate or tender. *Sensible* = reasonable / practical.
e *worthless* This means having no value. *Priceless* = very valuable.
f *alone* This means on your own, by yourself. *Lonely* = feeling unhappy because you are alone.

H Practice
a effect
b productive
c idea
d enthusiasm
e came up with
f employees
g Experiments
h expert

7 A short history of frozen food

A Introduction
1 a crystal / to defrost / to freeze / freezer / freezing / frozen / to thaw out
b They contain the letters *fr-*.
c 1 freezer
2 crystal
3 to freeze
4 to defrost / thaw out
5 frozen
6 freezing

d 1 crammed
2 to stuff
3 to preserve
4 naturalist
5 mushy
6 to keep

B Reading
1 a The Chinese
b In the Canadian Arctic
c It goes mushy. Slow-freezing forms large ice crystals which break up the flesh of the fish.
d 26 different kinds of frozen food were sold (to the public) from a freezer in a shop in Massachusetts.
2 a stuffing
b frozen
c naturalist
d preserve
e thawed out (defrosted *is possible*)
f froze
g mushy
h crystals
i freezing
j freezer
k crammed
l defrosted (*or* thawed out)

C Verbs + prepositions
a of (to smell *of*)
b in (to succeed *in* doing something)
c with (to fill something *with* something)
d on (to rely *on* something / someone)
e on (to depend *on* something / someone)
f for (to thank someone *for* (doing) something)
g for (to pay (money) *for* something)
h from (to suffer *from* an illness)

D Near synonyms
1 *appalling / awful / horrible* (= very bad)
appetising / delicious / tasty (= tasting good)
to fill / to pack / to stuff (= to put a lot of things into)
heaps / loads / piles (= large numbers, quantities of)
microscopic / minute / tiny (= very small)

2 a awful / appalling / horrible
  b tiny / microscopic / minute
  c stuffed / packed (You cannot *fill* clothes *into* something. You *fill* something *with* clothes.)
  d loads / piles / heaps
  e delicious / appetising / tasty

EXTENSION: Word stress
  a con'tent
  b 'desert
  c ob'ject
  d 'permit
  e pre'sent
  f 'refuse

E Materials
  a Shoes: leather (and rubber?)
  b Car wheel: metal and rubber (and plastic?)
  c Jug: pottery
  d Mirror: glass and wood
  e Sunglasses: metal or plastic (frames) and glass or plastic (lenses)
  f Trousers: cloth / material
  g Notebook: paper and metal or plastic

F Occupations
  a musi**cian**
  b guitar**ist**
  c window clean**er**
  d act**or**
  e biolog**ist**
  f politi**cian**
  g econom**ist**
  h direct**or**
  i company manag**er**
  j computer operat**or**

G Puzzle
  a defrost, freezer
  b tiny, minute
  c appalling, awful
  d content, desert
  e glass, plastic
  f actor
  g guitarist

8 Emails home

A Introduction
1 a 5
  b 7
  c 8
  d 6
  e 2
  f 1
  g 3
  h 9
  i 4
2 *Possible answers:*
  a I'm going to hire a bike and explore the area.
  b There is sand on the beach. / The beach is made of lovely golden sand.
  c We took sleeping bags and a tent so that we could camp.

B Reading
  a hectic
  b recovering
  c impressive
  d body clocks
  e harbour
  f hire
  g spa
  h cut costs
  i backpackers

C Verb-noun collocations
1 cut: bread / costs / prices / a scene from a film / taxes
  find: the answer to a question / a cure for a disease / the solution to a problem / your way (somewhere)
  have: the answer / a bath / a break / breakfast / dinner / a holiday / a rest / a shower
2 a have a break
  b cut several scenes
  c find a cure

  d find my way
  e had a holiday
  f find the answer
  g cut their prices

EXTENSION 1: Idioms with *cut*
  a 3
  b 2
  c 5
  d 1
  e 4

D Phrasal verbs with *set*
  a set up
  b set about
  c set off
  d set back
  e setting down

E 1 Adverbs meaning 'completely'
  a fast asleep
  b wide open
  c dead easy
  d flat broke (*broke* = having no money)
  e dead quiet

F Comparative adjectives
  a busier
  b more exhausted
  c better
  d happier
  e hotter
  f more impressive
  g lovelier
  h newer
  i safer
  j more special
  k stranger
  l tireder / more tired

G Practice
  a wonderful / amazing
  b exhausted
  c body clock
  d hire
  e area
  f camp
  g sleeping bag
  h tent
  i beach
  j amazing / wonderful

9 Rowing across the Atlantic

A Introduction
1 a 10
  b 1
  c 6

d 3
e 8
f 7
g 4
h 5
i 2
j 9

B Reading
 a completed
 b reception
 c sensation
 d developed
 e phobia
 f pulled out
 g rowing
 h ups and downs
 i loneliness
 j misery

C Related words
1 a beautiful, beautifully
 b destroy, destructive, destructively
 c instruct, instructive
 d know, knowledgeable, knowledgeably
 e lonely
 f miserable, miserably
 g peaceful, peacefully
 h sense, sensational, sensationally
2 a instructive
 b knowledgeable
 c sensational
 d peaceful
 e miserable
 f destructive
 g beautiful
 h lonely

D Adjective-noun collocations
1 hard: decision / drugs / luck / work
 heavy: rain / smoker / traffic / work
 strong: coffee / leader / opinion / taste / wind
2 a heavy smoker
 b taste, strong
 c hard decision
 d hard luck
 e traffic, heavier
 f strong leader

EXTENSION: Adjectives ending in -ed and -ing
1 a excited
 b amazing

2 *Bored* is how you feel. *Boring* describes something (or somebody) that gives you this feeling.
3 a interesting
 b relaxed
 c tiring
 d annoying
 e depressed

E Phrasal verbs
 a pulled out
 b carry on
 c get up
 d ran (her) down
 e going on

F Phrasal verbs with *pull*
1 a pull down
 b pull off
 c pull out
 d pull in
 e pull through
 f pull off
 g pull out
2 a pulled off
 b (has) pulled through
 c pulled down
 d pull out
 e pulled out

G People
 a 5
 b 7
 c 6
 d 8
 e 10
 f 4
 g 9
 h 2
 i 3
 j 1

H Puzzle

```
         k
a      P H O B I A
b      D E S T R O Y
c    H A R D
d      P E A C E
e      R E S I D E N T
f  R E C E P T I O N
g      S T R O N G
h      M I S E R Y
i      H E A V Y
j      A N N O Y E D
```

10 A journey to remember

A Introduction
1 a 7

b 10
c 1
d 6
e 9
f 4
g 2
h 5
i 8
j 3

B Reading
 a deserted
 b timidly
 c confidently
 d honked
 e proudly
 f founded
 g Tragically
 h destroyed
 i contrast
 j purchased

C Related words
1 a confident, confidence
 b desperate, desperation
 c fluent, fluency
 d frequent, frequency
 e particular
 f proud, pride
 g timid, timidity
 h tragic, tragedy
2 a desperate
 b tragedy
 c timidity, confidence
 d particular
 e fluent
 f frequent
 g proud

D Adjective-noun collocations
1 common: effect / flower / name / sight
 lasting: effect / impression / relationship
 sharp: bend / contrast / increase / knife / teeth
2 a a common flower
 b a lasting relationship
 c a common name
 d a sharp bend

EXTENSION 1: Verbs ending in -en
 a shorten
 b straighten
 c widen
 d tighten
 e sweeten
 f loosen

103

E Verb-noun collocations

1 catch: a bus / a coach / a plane / a train

drive: a bus / a car / a coach / a taxi / a train

miss: a boat / a bus / a coach / a plane / a train

ride: a bicycle / a horse / a motorbike

travel by: bicycle / boat / bus / car / coach / motorbike / plane / taxi / train

Note: *travel on horseback, take a taxi*

2 a 5, miss
   b 3, travel
   c 1, bicycle
   d 6, catch
   e 2, drive
   f 4, ride

Extension 2: Expressions with *catch*

   a got
   b attract / get
   c captured
   d hear
   e found

F Travel nouns

   a airport, plane, pilot
   b port, boat, sailor
   c bus station, bus, driver
   d railway station, train, driver

G Compound adjectives

1 a handmade / hand-woven
   b fast-moving / strong-looking
   c curly-haired / long-legged

2 a government-financed
   b egg-shaped
   c warm-hearted
   d slow-moving
   e sweet-smelling
   f left-handed

H Practice

   a fluently
   b railway
   c missed
   d train
   e deserted
   f catch
   g dark
   h attention
   i timidly
   j driver

11 Claiming compensation

A Introduction

1 a 5
   b 8
   c 10
   d 1
   e 9
   f 3
   g 4
   h 2
   i 6
   j 7

B Reading

1 a entitled
   b legal
   c injuries
   d claim
   e fees
   f blaming
   g pavements
   h fault
   i compensation
   j rise

2 a They may be able to *claim compensation*.
   b They are offering *legal assistance*.
   c If they *lose their claim*.
   d They *blame the school*.
   e To *make money*.
   f The customers of *insurance companies* usually pay the money.

C Verb-noun collocations

1 make: fun of someone / a joke / money / notes / a profit

pay: fees / money / rent / tax(es)

take: advice / care / an exam / a joke / medicine / notes / responsibility (for)

2 a takes advice
   b medicine to take
   c made a small profit
   d make fun, take a joke
   e pay rent
   f Take care

D Expressions with *go* + adjective

   a 4
   b 7
   c 2
   d 5

   e 8
   f 3
   g 1
   h 6

EXTENSION 1: Colour expressions

   a blue
   b green
   c black (and) white
   d red
   e White

E *Blame* and *fault*

2 a I blame John for the accident.
   b They said the disaster was the government's fault.
   c Don't blame me.
   d (I think) it's Rachel's fault / it was Rachel's fault.

F Formal and informal words

   a 3
   b 5
   c 4
   d 1
   e 2
   f 1

Extension 2: Meanings of *get*

   a buy
   b understand
   c become
   d receive
   e arrive
   f earn

G Puzzle

   a earn, buy
   b assistance
   c injure
   d profit, living
   e joke, advice
   f bald, grey
   g green
   h red

12 Odd news

A Introduction
1 **a** 4
b 8
c 7
d 6
e 10
f 9
g 3
h 1
i 5
j 2

B Reading
a impressed
b ingredient
c equivalent
d cosmetics
e alternative
f consists
g technician
h performance
i prepare
j discovery

C Related words
1 **a** discovery
b important, importantly
c inclusion, inclusive
d necessity, necessarily
e supplement, supplementary
f preparation, prepared
g reduction
h safety, safely
2 **a** safety
b preparation
c reduction
d important
e supplement
f necessity

D Adjective-noun collocations
1 **general**: election / interest / knowledge / rule
normal: behaviour / day / price / relations / way
public: health / holiday / interest / knowledge / opinion / relations
2 **a** the normal price
b a general election
c the normal way
d public opinion
e general knowledge
f a public holiday

E Nationalities
a Japan, Japanese
b Austria, Austrian
c America / the United States, American
d Chinese
e Egyptian
f Canada
g Swedish
h Spain
i Dutch
j Iraqi
k Thailand

F Adjectives + prepositions
a for
b to
c for
d for
e to
f about
g of
h to
i for
j at

EXTENSION: Adjectives starting with a...
a the sleeping passengers
b the burning / blazing car
c The living creatures
d The floating ship

G Homophones
a wait
b weak
c our
d symbol
e lead
f sew

H Puzzle

```
                 k
a    C O N S I S T
b            N O R M A L
c            G R A T E F U L
d        P E R F O R M A N C E
e    A B L A Z E
f            D U T C H
g    T E C H N I C I A N
h            R E D U C T I O N
i        G E N E R A L
j    C O S M E T I C S
```

13 The ideal sheepdog

A Introduction
1 **a** 4
b 8
c 1
d 5
e 6
f 3
g 9
h 10
i 2
j 7

B Reading
1 **a** trained
b cage
c wander
d agriculture
e pet
f herd
g tough
h force
i staring
j stubborn
k train
2 **a** In Texas at the home of a trainer
b It gathered chickens together and kept them in one place.
c England and Scotland
d He is a dog trainer. / He trains border collies.
e They like to work all the time.

C Animals
1 **Pets**: cat / dog / horse / monkey (?) / rabbit
Working animals: camel / dog / donkey / elephant / horse
Farm animals and birds: chicken / cow / deer / duck / pig / sheep / turkey
Wild animals and birds: camel / deer / dog / duck / elephant / giraffe / horse / lion / monkey / rabbit / tiger / turkey
3 **a** cat / kitten
b cow / calf
c dog / puppy
d horse / foal
e lion / cub
f pig / piglet
g sheep / lamb

EXTENSION: Animal idioms
a a cold fish
b a dark horse
c an early bird
d a busy bee
e a guinea pig
f the top dog

D Phrasal verbs
1 a round up
b work out
c come across
d lie down
e work out
f find out
2 a working out
b found out
c rounded (them) up
d lie down
e came across
f work out

E Phrasal verbs with *come*
a came up against
b come up
c came out with
d came round
e Come on!
f come from

F 'Seeing' verbs
a see / watch
b see
c staring at / looking at
d gazing
e notice / see
f Look at

G Puzzle

```
          I
a      D A R K
b      G A Z E
c      T R A I N E R
d      F I S H
e        C U B
f    S T U B B O R N
g    C A L F
h    K I T T E N
i        P U P P Y
j    S T A R E
k    C A G E
```

14 Freak weather

A Introduction
1 a 6
b 5
c 8
d 2
e 1

f 7
g 4
h 3
2 a sunset
b horizon
c cliff
d coast
e bay
f snow-capped peak

B Reading
1 a flabbergasted
b sunset
c convinced
d glimpse
e incredible
f coast
g bay
h cliffs
i Mirages
j invert
k horizon
2 a 3
b 5
c 2
d 1
e 4

C People
a fisherman
b expert
c resident
d islander
e passenger
f sailor

EXTENSION: More people
a villager
b cyclist
c shop assistant
d customer / shopper
e victim
f librarian
g criminal / law-breaker
h gardener
i decorator / painter
j gambler

D Near synonyms
1 a few / several / some
appear / become visible /
come into view
calm / peaceful / quiet
cause / create / produce
clear / on view / visible
disappear / fade / vanish
2 a calm (peaceful *and* quiet
are also possible)
b visible
c cause / create / produce

d a few / several (some *is
also possible*)
e appeared / became
visible / came into view
f disappeared / vanished

E Phrasal verbs with *make*
1 Meaning **b** is correct.
2 a make up
b make up
c make for
d make off
3 a make up
b made off
c made up
d made for
e making it all up

F Place prepositions
a on
b up / down
c in, over
d around / close to / near /
in front of / behind
e on
f at / on

G Puzzle
a sure, certain, convinced
b mirage
c sunset
d cliffs
e horizon
f expert
g visible
h quiet, calm

15 Old tyres

A Introduction
1 a 6
b 7
c 10
d 8
e 9
f 2
g 1
h 3
i 4
j 5

B Reading

1 a landfill sites
   b ban
   c estimated
   d recycled
   e converted
   f surfaces
   g fuel
   h dispose of
   i illegal
   j breeding grounds
2 a European countries
   b up to 100,000
   c 18 per cent
   d Spain
   e in the sea

C Related words

1 a concern, concerned
   b environment,
      environmentally
   c estimate
   d expense, expensively
   e popularity, popularly
   f science, scientific,
      scientifically
   g success, succeed,
      successfully
2 a succeed
   b popularity
   c environment
   d concerns
   e estimate
   f Science
   g expensively

D Phrasal verbs with *fall*

1 Meaning **c**
2 a fall for
   b fall behind
   c fall through
   d fall down
   e fall out
3 a fallen through
   b fell behind
   c fell for
   d fell down
   e fall out

E Verbs + prepositions

1 a believe in
   b approve of, agree with
   c converted into
   d object to
   e insist on
   f belongs to, borrow it from
   g choose between
   h know very little about

F Prefixes

1 a return: take back
   b reread: read again
   c rewound: wound back
   d redo: do again
   e rebuild: build again
2 a 5
   b 6
   c 7
   d 1
   e 8
   f 4
   g 2
   h 3
3 a postponed
   b misbehaved
   c semi-detached
   d bilingual
   e overcharge
   f monotonous
   g antisocial
   h undercooked

EXTENSION

   a a monosyllable
   b a bigamist
   c postscript
   d misfortune
   e an antidote

G Practice

   a tyres
   b fuel
   c oil
   d recycled
   e disposed of
   f environment
   g temperature
   h smoke

16 Volcanoes

A Introduction

1 a 6
   b 5
   c 2
   d 9
   e 10
   f 8
   g 1
   h 11
   i 7
   j 4
   k 3

B Reading

1 a active
   b at risk
   c erupt
   d liquid
   e flowing
   f fragments
   g climate
   h disrupted
   i predict
   j likely
   k monitor
2 a mantle
   b crust
   c magma
   d ash
   e lava

C Related words

1 a action / activity, act,
      actively
   b disruption, disruptive
   c eruption
   d explosion, explode,
      explosively
   e prediction, predictable,
      predictably
   f severity, severely
   g threat, threatening,
      threateningly
   h violence, violent
   i volcanic
2 a disruption
   b violence
   c exploded
   d threat
   e predictable
   f severity

**D Adjectives and their
   opposites**

1 a 3
   b 4
   c 7
   d 8
   e 2
   f 5
   g 6
   h 1
2 a inactive
   b unusual
   c unlikely
   d non-violent
   e unpredictable
   f impossible
   g inexpensive
   h impractical
3 a non-violent
   b unpredictable
   c impractical
   d unlikely
   e unusual
   f inexpensive

E Collocations: 'Size' adjectives + nouns

1 **deep**: feeling / hole / water
  small: area / book / business / change / country / hole / majority / number
  thick: book / hair / layer / line / pullover / shirt
  thin: book / hair / layer / line / pullover / shirt
  vast: area / country / majority / number

2 **a** deep feeling
  b a thin shirt
  c the vast majority
  d small change
  e a thick pullover
  f a small business

EXTENSION: Idioms with 'size' adjectives

  a 4
  b 1
  c 5
  d 3
  e 2

F Plural of nouns ending in -o

1 **a** Other examples: *cargoes, echoes, potatoes*
  b Other examples: *euros, memos, pianos, rhinos*

2 **a** heroes
  b studios
  c kilos
  d videos
  e discos

G Practice

  a impossible
  b eruption
  c practical
  d lava
  e volcanic
  f measure
  g safer
  h volcano
  i prevent
  j dangers

17 New carrots

A Introduction

1 **a** 7
  b 10
  c 5
  d 1
  e 2

  f 9
  g 6
  h 3
  i 4
  j 8

B Reading

1 **a** original
  b on sale
  c natural
  d commercial
  e spread
  f vision
  g bunch
  h seeds
  i influence
  j artificial

2 **a** F There were many different colours in the past.
  b F They are orange on the inside.
  c F Betacarotene improves vision in dim light. (*Anthocyanin* may help prevent heart disease.)
  d T
  e F Over 90% of carrot varieties have been lost.

C Related words

1 **a** encouragement, encouraging
  b entire
  c influence, influential
  d origin / originality, originate, originally
  e prevention, preventable / preventive (*or* preventative)
  f store
  g various / varied

2 **a** entire
  b prevention
  c encouragement
  d various
  e influences
  f originally
  g store

D Vegetables and colours

2 *Aubergines* are usually purple.
  Beans can be many different colours.
  Broccoli is green, or green and purple.
  Cabbage is green or purple.
  Cauliflower is white.

Courgettes are green or yellow.
Garlic is white.
Onions are white, or red and white.
Peas are green.
Potatoes are white on the inside and brown on the outside.
Mushrooms are white.

E Adjective-noun collocations

1 **dark**: b, g
  dim: c, d, f
  dull: a, e, f

2 **dark**: colour / eyes / glasses / hair
  dim: light / memory / student
  dull: colour / hair / pain / story / student / weather

3 **a** dim memories
  b dull pain
  c dim light
  d weather, dull
  e dark hair and eyes
  f dark glasses

4 **a** bright / clear / interesting
  b bright
  c sharp
  d fair / light
  e interesting
  f light / bright
  g clear

F Numbers and words

  a four thousand
  b the thirteen hundreds
  c nineteen ninety-nine
  d twenty per cent
  e the twentieth century
  f nineteen oh three
  g two hundred and eighty-seven

EXTENSION: Words and numbers

  a 27.5%
  b 1762
  c 14,911
  d $^3/_4$
  e 820445
  f 6.45
  g 13th June
  h 1.75

G Puzzle

```
               k
a        C A U L I F L O W E R
b          B R I G H T
c      C E N T U R Y
d          O R I G I N
e            I N F L U E N C E
f              D I M
g      B U N C H
h      V A R I E D
i          P E A S
j      D U L L
```

18 The writer

A Introduction

1 a 5
  b 8
  c 4
  d 10
  e 2
  f 9
  g 1
  h 6
  i 3
  j 7

B Reading

1 a exchange
  b turned into
  c entertain
  d lively
  e pause
  f background
  g distant
  h click
  i inhabitants
  j primitive

2 a 5
  b 1
  c 6
  d 2
  e 3
  f 4

C Related words

1 a creator, create, creative,
    creatively
  b description, descriptive
  c distance, distantly
  d entertainment, entertainer,
    entertaining, entertainingly
  e inhabit, inhabited,
    uninhabited
  f intelligence, unintelligent,
    intelligently
  g laugh

2 a entertainment

  b laughed
  c uninhabited
  d create
  e distance
  f description

D Verb-noun collocations

1 **earn**: a living / money /
    wages
    gain: experience / weight
    win: the lottery / money /
    a prize / a race / a war

2 a won the lottery
  b gained (so much) weight
  c earn (my) living
  d won (several) prizes
  e earn (very high) wages
  f gained (valuable)
    experience

**EXTENSION: Countable and
uncountable nouns**

1 a U
  b C
  c C
  d U

2 a 8
  b 6
  c 7
  d 5
  e 3
  f 1
  g 4
  h 2

E Onomatopoeic words

  a splash
  b growled
  c whispering
  d crash
  e creaked
  f jingling

F Phrasal verbs with _go_

  a go without
  b goes off
  c gone / been through
  d going down with
  e went by

G Puzzle

  a splash
  b wood
  c pause
  d gain
  e lively
  f create
  g inhabitant
  h click

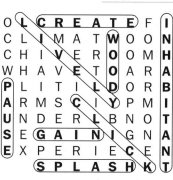

```
O L C R E A T E F I
C L I M A T W O O N
C H I V E R O O M H
W H A V E T O A R A
P L I T I L D O R B
A R M S C I Y P M I
U N D E R L B N O T
S E G A I N G N A N
E X P E R I E C E T
S P L A S H K T
```

19 An unusual suggestion

A Introduction

1 a 3
  b 8
  c 5
  d 10
  e 6
  f 7
  g 2
  h 9
  i 4
  j 1

B Reading

1 a crowded
  b scruffy
  c denim
  d shopping mall
  e obvious
  f panic
  g charity shop
  h scared
  i sleeve
  j by mistake

2 a brown
  b a (scruffy old) baseball cap
  c in a shopping mall
  d He asked him if he had got /
    bought the shirt at a
    charity shop.
  e Steve
  f on the sleeve
  g He wanted to buy it
    back from the boy.

**C Clothes and parts of
clothes**

1 A jacket
  B trainers
  C shirt
  D socks
  E trousers
  F baseball cap

2 g zip
h sleeve
i collar
j button
k cuff
l belt
m pocket
n leg
o lace

D Idioms with *eye*
1 *I was afraid to take my eyes off him* ... Meaning **a**
I caught his eye ...
Meaning **c**
2 a 3
b 5
c 1
d 2
e 4
3 a see eye to eye
b up to my eyes
c turns a blind eye
d pull the wool over her eyes
e keeping your eye on

EXTENSION: More things you can wear
a glasses
b ring
c bracelet
d nail varnish
e earring
f lipstick
g necklace
h watch

E Adjective order
1 a ✔
b scruffy old baseball cap
c big blue denim shirt
2 a ✔
b beautiful pear-shaped silver earrings
c short dark straight hair
d wonderful new French trainers
e small black leather bag

F Meanings of *look*
1 a 6
b 5
c 4
d 2
e 1
f 3
2 a Look out!
b look like
c looked it up

d looked
e look on the bright side

G Practice
a blue denim
b charity shop
c mistake
d café
e boy
f panic
g away
h scared
i arrest

20 Random acts of kindness

A Introduction
1 a 7
b 9
c 5
d 3
e 8
f 6
g 2
h 4
i 1

B Reading
1 a tollbooth
b fare
c random
d spotted
e jotted (it) down
f mops
g rundown
h frail
i impulse
2 Meaning **b** is correct.
3 a 4
b 5
c 1
d 3
e 2

C Word groups
1 a vehicle
b language
c furniture
d instrument
e flower
2 *Other possible examples:*
a motorbike, van, tractor, truck, coach
b accent, punctuation, grammar, vocabulary
c desk, bookshelf, wardrobe, chest of drawers
d guitar, saxophone,

clarinet, flute
e daffodil, carnation, lily, orchid

D American English
1 a 6, drive
b 1, bucket
c 2, plonk
d 3, *no equivalent word*
e 4, year seven pupil
f 5, cashier
2 a a check
b to practise (in British English *practice* is the noun)

E Describing periods of time
a warm summer afternoon
b cool autumn evening
c bright / sunny spring morning
d long summer holiday
e cold December night

F Phrasal verbs with *hand*
1 a hand over
b hand out
c hand in
d hand back
2 a hand in
b handed it back
c hand out
d hand over

EXTENSION: Idioms with *hand*
1 a 4
b 3
c 2
d 1
2 a out of hand
b lend you a hand
c Hands off
d my hands full

G Puzzle

```
                    j
a   B U C K E T
b         F L O W E R
c     I M P U L S E
d         T E L L E R
e               B A C K
f   R A N D O M
g             J O T
h   S P O T
i         V E H I C L E S
```

Review 1

1 Related words
b privacy
c growth
d visitors
e reality
f silence
g electrician
h valuable

2 Verb-noun collocations
a lose
b save
c lose
d waste
e keeping
f held
g spent
h win

3 *Make* and *do*
a made
b making
c do
d make
e do
f make
g make

4 Adjectives
a electric
b expensive
c economical
d cheap
e irresponsible

5 Adjective opposites
a unattractive
b impolite
c immature
d illegal
e unintentional

6 Odd one out
b piano *The other words are parts of a mobile phone.*
c track *The other words are types of music.*
d band *The other words are types of recordings.*
e angry *The other words have similar meanings.*
f number plate *The others are American English words.*

Review 2

1 Verb-noun collocations
a find someone guilty
b find your way
c cut prices
d have breakfast
e cut taxes
f have a shower

2 Adjective-noun collocations
a leading
b concrete
c brilliant
d artificial
e long-term
f inspiring

3 Phrasal verbs
a set off
b come up with
c carrying out
d put up with
e set up
f carry on

4 Related words
a explorer
b theoretical
c productivity
d concentration
e brilliance

5 Prepositions
a on
b with
c in
d from
e for
f of
g for
h in

Review 3

1 Related words
a destruction
b knowledge
c performance
d proudly
e reduction
f safety

2 Adjective-noun collocations
a strong coffee
b sharp increase
c public opinion
d common sight
e normal behaviour

f lasting effect
g heavy rain, hard luck

3 Verb-noun collocations
a miss
b make
c take
d catch
e travel
f ride
g pay

4 Choose the correct word
a annoyed
b for
c green
d of
e fault
f weak
g blame

5 Compound adjectives
b short-haired
c home-cooked
d healthy-looking
e blue-eyed
f heart-shaped

Review 4

1 Phrasal verbs
a work out
b make out
c made up
d fallen out
e fell down

2 More phrasal verbs
a come from
b come round
c come up with
d came up against
e come up

3 Related words
a explosion
b disruption
c threatening
d severely
e popularity
f prediction
g environmental
h eruption

4 Prepositions
a belong to
b approve of
c on the coast
d object to
e agree with
f over the house

5 True or false?

a F A *cold fish* is someone who shows no feelings. Someone who has a secret life is called a *dark horse*.

b F A *guinea pig* is someone who is used in an experiment. Someone who never stops doing things is called a *busy bee*.

c T

d F A young horse is a *foal*. A *lamb* is a young sheep.

e T

f F They can speak two languages.

g F It has been cooked too much.

h F *radios*

i F a *dormant* volcano

j T

6 Confusing words

a notice

b thick

c small

d see

e vast

f stare

Review 5

1 Related words

a creative

b laughter

c inhabitant

d encouragement

e prevention

f description

g influential

h originality

i entertainment

2 Phrasal verbs

a go without

b hand out

c go by

d handed it back

e gone down

f going through

g gone off

3 Adjective-noun collocations

a dark (glasses)

b dull (pain)

c dim (memory)

d dull (film)

e dark (brown hair)

4 Adjective order

a a fantastic, silver-grey American car

b a tall green glass vase

c short dark curly hair

d an old brown woollen pullover

e an incredible large gold ring

5 True or false?

a T

b F It makes a *splash*.

c T

d F *To pull the wool over someone's eyes* means to deceive them.

e F *To see eye to eye with someone* means to agree with them.

f F The British English for *driveway* is *drive*.

g T

h T

i T

j F A *collar* is part of a shirt, blouse, dress, jacket or coat. It is the part that goes round your neck.